Spiritual Intelligence

A Lion Book
an imprint of
Lion Hudson plc
Wilkinson House, Jordan Hill Road,
Oxford OX2 8DR, England
www.lionhudson.com
ISBN 978 0 7459 5321 2 (UK)
ISBN 978 0 8254 7874 1 (US)

Distributed by:
UK: Marston Book Services, PO Box 269, Abingdon, Oxon, OX14 4YN
USA: Trafalgar Square Publishing, 814 N. Franklin Street, Chicago, IL 60610
USA: Christian Market: Kregel Publications, PO Box 2607, Grand Rapids, MI 49501

First edition 2009
10 9 8 7 6 5 4 3 2 1 0

Acknowledgments
Every effort has been made to trace and acknowledge copyright holders of all the quotations
included. We apologize for any errors or omissions that may remain, and would ask those
concerned to contact the publishers, who will ensure that full acknowledgment is made in
the future.
Scripture quotations are from: pp. 29, 37, 47, 50, 64, 114, 119, 152, 153 New Revised Standard
Version published by HarperCollins Publishers, copyright © 1989 by the Division of Christian
Education of the National Council of the Churches of Christ in the USA, and are used by
permission. All rights reserved; pp. 54, 124, 187 The Message. Copyright © 1993, 1994, 1995,
1996, 2000, 2001, 2002. Used by permission of NavPress Publishing Group; pp. 58, 156, 157,
176, 184: The New King James Version copyright © 1982, 1979 by Thomas Nelson, Inc.; p. 60
Holy Bible, New Living Translation, copyright © 1996. Used by permission of Tyndale House
Publishers, Inc., Wheaton, Illinois 60189. All rights reserved; pp. 105, 107, 168; The Holy
Bible, English Standard Version, published by HarperCollins Publishers, copyright © 2001
Crossway Bibles, a division of Good News Publishers. Used by permission. All rights reserved;
p. 159 NEW AMERICAN STANDARD BIBLE®, Copyright © 1960, 1962, 1963, 1968, 1971,
1972, 1973, 1975, 1977, 1995 by The Lockman Foundation. Used by permission.
p. 30: 'Leisure' by William Henry Davies. Used with permission of K. P. Griffin, Trustee of Mrs
H. M. Davies Will Trust; p. 33: Extract from *The Dhammapada: The Sayings of the Buddha*, ed./
trans. Thomas Byron, © Random House, 1976; p. 66: lyrics taken from 'From Auschwitz to
Ipswich' by Jarvis Cocker, released by Rough Trade Records. Used with permission of Warner/
Chappell Music Ltd.

A catalogue record for this book is available
from the British Library

Typeset in 11/12 Arno Pro
Printed and bound in Great Britain by CPI Cox & Wyman, Reading.

Spiritual Intelligence
A new way of being

Brian Draper

LION

For Mercy,
my daughter and friend

Contents

Acknowledgments

For the last couple of years, I have worked inter-dependently with MCA, a business consultancy in Winchester which is seeking to model a new way of being to the private and public sectors.

Some of the ideas in this book have arisen through the conversations, the moments of clarity, the meetings and workshops, the failures and successes and epiphanies we've shared - as we have sought to help ordinary people unleash their extraordinary potential through spiritual intelligence.

Thanks to Alison for your energy and encouragement, to Nick for your assuring presence, to Sarah for your revolutionary heart and your enduring kindness, to Andrew for profound times of creative breakthrough and spiritual companionship, to Ellen for helping me laugh at myself, and to Michael, a planting of the LORD for the display of his splendour.

The idea for the icons arose first when I worked at the London Institute for Contemporary Christianity, and I am grateful to Mark Greene for letting me explore these further on my own, and for the continued friendship, support and encouragement of all the staff there.

Thank you to James Evans for your soulful support; for your courage and inspiration in seeking to restore the young people you serve so passionately, and for giving them hope. You are writing a far more eloquent story of spiritual intelligence through your life's work, than I am with this book.

Finally, I remain indebted to Kats, Eden and Mercy for giving me the head space and heart space without which a writer cannot write, a thinker cannot think, and a human cannot be.

Introduction

In our quick-fix consumer culture, we've grown used to getting what we want, when we want it (even if we can't afford it).

You can even buy a fake university degree from the Internet if you really want the prestige of hanging a phoney certificate on your wall. Most of us don't go that far, of course! But for many people, to one degree or another, it's all about appearances; how you get there in life matters less than *looking like* you've arrived.

Ironically, this attitude can take us quite a long way. We begin to excel as we hone and nurture our 'life skills' and try to stand out from the crowd, as if we'd been born into one great competition. We tell ourselves that this is really the way to go. The trouble is, we end up becoming experts in the art of illusion, not the art of life – we give others the illusion that we're winning, that we're really going places, and we begin to live under that illusion (or delusion) ourselves.

How big is your house? How fast is your car? Which school do your children go to? Wow, you're really quite *someone*! I need to work harder to keep up with you…

Our hearts swell with pride when we see others glancing in admiration as we overtake them on the road of life – *and we begin to believe the hype.* We tell ourselves that we really *must* be someone (even if we don't truly believe it deep down), because everyone else thinks so too… and so we set ourselves off on a journey that demands that we live up to that billing – to be the person others think we are. For the rest of our days, we have to hold on for dear life, in case we are found out.

The trouble is, we can travel so far on this journey, but ultimately we get to a point where we can go no further. We reach a dead end, without ever realizing our true potential – our infinite potential. Even the CEOs of the most successful businesses probably sense, in their hearts, that they can only get so far by playing a role, acting the big cheese, putting on a mask and driving themselves and their workers so hard that they forget who they were in the first place.

We end up wearing multiple masks as we struggle to be liked, loved and respected, and not 'found out'... and so we build up layers like limescale on a kettle, until we forget who we were ever created to be in the first place.

Which reminds me: who *were* we created to be in the first place?

* * *

Stop to think
Remember the carefree days when you were so young that you had 'achieved' nothing in life, except for playing around and building tree houses and collecting worms and completing jigsaw puzzles...? Who were you then?

Stop to think for a moment. Listen to that child's voice speaking to you. What did it sound like? What was it saying?

When did you begin to accumulate the layers in your life? When you began to pass or fail exams? When you were accepted or rejected for job interviews? How did those experiences shape you? Can you remember when you were asked out or rejected by your first love? How did that leave you feeling?

In what ways did you either learn to defend your sense of self, or to attack others in order to grow that sense of self?

What was the essence of you, before you learned how to make others happy, or to defend yourself in the playground? What was the essence of you, before you found a talent that would impress other people?

* * *

We relentlessly compare ourselves with each other, only to find ourselves wanting – wanting more and more. You might want your neighbour's husband or wife, or their lifestyle, or their luck in life... But why? What is it that we *really* want, if we are truly honest? That is the most important thing we can begin to awaken to.

Do we want to be successful? Do we wish to be someone? Of course we do. And that is only natural. But it's the way we channel these impulses that will ultimately help to determine who we really are.

Your heart is reaching out for more because it knows, deep down, that there *is* so much more to who you really are, and to what you can do with your life. Your heart is aching both to realize and *recall* who you really are. It yearns to reconnect with the reason you were created in the first place. It longs to find the 'someone' you really are: the unique you, with a unique fingerprint and a unique way of touching the world and leaving your mark upon it; the priceless one-in-six-billion you, with a unique iris, and a unique way of seeing the world and acting upon what you see.

Our story has far more potential than we realize. It's about so much more than the stuff we accumulate, the numbers of zeros on our salary, and all of the usual things we put our security in. You cannot buy yourself a good story, nor embellish it with false trappings; hold your story up to the light of life and it will not be about the external things we are so often seduced by.

So what kind of story will people tell at your funeral? What kind of story will those who have worked with you, lived with you, loved you, really tell about the way you have lived and loved? You have the chance – before that funeral! – to craft something much richer, deeper and more beautiful than the usual script; but only if you dare to awaken to the possibilities – and to the harder fact that you are, at the moment, asleep. And that is where we must begin on this journey.

This is no quick fix, no off-the-shelf consumerist spiritual lifestyle choice. It's subversively free of charge, as the best things in life really are. But it also comes at great cost: the cost of lifelong commitment, dedication, passion, sacrifice and selfless, self-giving love.

What is 'spiritual intelligence'?

The spiritual writer Evelyn Underhill wrote, 'We cannot say that there is a separate "mystical sense" which some men have and some men have not, but rather that *every human soul has a certain latent capacity for God, and that in some capacity is realised with an astonishing richness.*'[1]

Spiritual intelligence is for us all, because it forms part of our total intelligence, our whole being. Yet we so rarely access it – either because we have succumbed to the secular impulse of the last two centuries, which suggests (at best) that spirituality should be left to religious people in churches or synagogues, mosques or temples, or (at worst) because we believe it plays no part in our scientific, secular age.

Most of us live such busy lives that we rarely take time to reflect on the riches buried in our hearts and in our traditions – riches that help us to discover who we really are, and to find meaning and purpose within our seemingly random, fragmented and ordinary existence; riches that help us to make those soulful reconnections that so many of us, deep down, yearn to make – with the world around us, with each other, with our selves, and with the higher power often called God.

In the year 2000, the Oxford academic, philosopher and spiritual writer Danah Zohar coined the phrase 'spiritual intelligence'. She suggested that it forms the central part of our intelligence, the part in which our values and beliefs are nurtured and in which we can work towards realizing our full potential as created beings. We have, for so long, focused on rational intelligence (IQ) as a way of improving ourselves and making our way in life; yet that is only a part of the story. Daniel Goleman introduced 'emotional intelligence' in more recent days, and has helped businesses and organizations to reflect on how their people can learn to manage their emotions and work more effectively and sensitively with others. More recently still, Zohar has argued that our spiritual intelligence can help bring meaning and purpose to our work and the world we inhabit.

She writes, 'So many of us today live lives of wounded fragmentation. We long for what the poet T. S. Eliot called a "further union, a deep communion", but we find little resource within our ego-bound selves or within the existing symbols or institutions of our culture... SQ is the intelligence that rests in that deep part of the self that is connected to wisdom from beyond the ego, or conscious mind; it is the intelligence with which we not only recognise existing values, but with which we creatively discover new values."[2]

I do not seek, in this book, to explain her reasoning or theories, but to use the opportunities afforded by the very idea of spiritual intelligence to explore what it means to embark on a journey of transformation – a journey that includes both contemplation and action in equal measure.

How to use this book: four journeys of increasing depth, through four icons

I have divided the book into four sections that comprise four separate 'journeys', each of which goes a little deeper into our spiritual intelligence. We start with level one: 'We are where we are.' At this level, we look very simply at becoming more aware of who we are and how we might awaken to the richer possibilities of life. Level two takes us on a journey of awakening to 'the false self' – the identity we create for ourselves through the relentless chattering of our ego-driven minds. In the third section, we explore 'the true self'. Who are we, really, deep down, and how can we find our 'sweet spot' – that part of us, that essence or core, from which we might live more effortlessly, more joyfully, more effectively? Finally, we consider what it means to live in 'flow', a mysterious place where we don't need all the answers, in which life as we know it begins to be replaced by a whole, new way of being.

Each 'journey' is divided into four stages (which are the same each time): 'awakening', 'seeing afresh', 'living the change' and 'passing it on'. I have used an icon for each. So, an alarm clock represents 'awakening'. An eye represents 'seeing afresh'. A paint brush and palette represent 'living the change' (to symbolize our unique, creative response to what we have learned about ourselves) and an arrow represents 'passing it on'.

The icons describe a process of spiritual growth, from awakening to new possibilities in life, to seeing your world through fresh eyes, to living differently and finally to passing on the benefits of your own transformation to those around you.

I have purposefully created a visual representation (the 'iconic grid') so that you can trace where you are on the journey, and understand more clearly the reasons for taking it one step at a time, in the order I have suggested. There are sixteen steps in all – effectively, you walk through the four icons at four different levels.

Of course, this is not a prescriptive journey, but a *descriptive* one. It is one way of trying to describe the processes we go through as we tap into our spiritual intelligence, to become more fully the people we were put on this earth to be. But I hope, as you read on, that you will begin to recognize times of awakening in your own life, as well as times when you start seeing things from a different perspective, times when you respond practically and times when you transmit the good news of your own transformation to others, like a positive contagion of hope.

A note on my own spiritual tradition

I write this book from my own perspective, so please read it as such. This is not a vast overview of different spiritualities, but a description of principles of spiritual intelligence that arise within each stage of the iconic journey. My own experience of spiritual awakening has arisen mainly through the Christian tradition, and so my examples flow more naturally from that source. But this book is not about becoming religious and neither is it seeking to persuade the reader to follow a particular line. Instead, I hope it provides wisdom for the journey of life, whoever you are, wherever you come from and whatever you believe.

Level 1

We are where we are

Chapter 1

Awakening

The great tragedy of life lies not in how much we suffer but in how much we miss. Human beings are born asleep, live asleep and die asleep... We have children asleep, raise children asleep, handle big business deals asleep, enter government office asleep, and die asleep. We never wake up. This is what spirituality is about: waking up.
Anthony de Mello[1]

Imagine you've been in a deep and, in many ways, a pleasant night's sleep. You are beginning to come round from that sleep, but you know you have a choice: wake up and face the challenges and opportunities of the day, or roll over, close your eyes, pull the duvet tight around you and slip back into unconsciousness. Sometimes it can be hard to drag yourself into the flow of life.

Let's face it: we all have a choice. We all face points in our lives, sacred moments in which we can awaken more vividly to life, if we choose to. Or we can slip back under the covers of our slumberous existence, afraid to grasp the reality of our present or to shape the possibilities of our future.

* * *

Do not press snooze

As we wake up each morning, we have a chance to awaken from so much more than just our physical sleep. We have the opportunity, as each new day presents itself, to wake up spiritually too. The trouble is, it's a struggle to become awake enough to what it means to be fully alive.

For a start, it's easy to turn the radio or TV on straight away, flood the room with the distraction of background noise, race to eat breakfast (if you're lucky) and press on with taking the children to school, or catching the train to work, or whatever you do – without stopping to fully engage your mind and heart and all your senses.

We usually start as we mean to go on. You can sleepwalk through the rest of the day, if you're not careful. I can sleepwalk through a week without thinking. A day becomes a week, a week becomes a month becomes a year becomes a life.

So try this: set your alarm five minutes earlier than usual. (That's all you need for now.) And when it goes off, do not press snooze but spend the extra five minutes at the start of your day *waking spiritually*. Spirituality is like a bridge between your being and your doing. And we need to attend to our being preferably before we move on to our doing.

Why not try the following for the next few days, as you wake up each morning:

Get out of bed and sit in a chair, or stand up if it helps.

■ Breathe in and out, slowly and deeply, and notice your breathing; take a moment to appreciate a new day and the gift of life. Do this for just a couple of minutes.

■ Become aware of the stillness around you, and notice any sounds that punctuate it; remember that everything you do today will come out of this stillness, and flow back into it again.

■ Look at your hands: remember that you are not just drifting through today, but helping to shape it from the start. Resolve to be a blessing to everyone you touch, physically, emotionally and spiritually today, and that the work of your hands will be honest, caring and good.

■ Now look at yourself in the mirror; and despite whether you like what you see or not, spend a few moments remembering that you are very much a part of the day's picture – not just a passive onlooker watching the rest of life unfold before you but playing your part as a character of great beauty and great potential.

* * *

A rare moment of awakening

The other day I went for an early morning run. I ran up a hill and came to the top. I could see the lane before me curving down on the other side for about 100 yards, and it was lined with trees and flowers – a beautiful sight. I resolved to appreciate this stretch as fully as I could as I ran through it. I looked at the flowers and the trees and thanked God for the beauty of the natural picture that surrounded me. And I felt an immediate reply come back: 'You are part of the beauty of this picture.'

* * *

What can we awaken from?

What, you may wonder, do I really need to awaken *from*? It's one thing to speak of waking from a spiritual 'sleep' – but what does that mean? Well, we're all sleepwalking (or racing) through life in one way or another – whether you're so busy at work that you're living for the weekend (when all you can do is recover), or so bored with what life seems to 'offer' in consumer culture, or lethargic, or stressed out, or driven by fear of failure or seduced by the promise of success...

Many things today are shutting us down, closing out the possibility of life in its fullness. Let's look at one: TV.

On average, we watch 4 to 5 hours of TV per day. Perhaps you're not an average Jo or Joanna; but most of us are. And if you're honest, most of what you watch is like moving wallpaper, drawing you in, zoning you out. 'TV is an animation of the triumph of the blasé,' wrote the self-styled 'alternative US tour guide' Speed Leitch. He's probably right.

Admittedly, there are some wonderful programmes on TV: educational, informative, entertaining. But do you ever tune in *just* to the programme you wish to watch, and then switch off when it's over? Probably not. Most of us will leave the TV on and let it radiate its presence, night after night, perhaps with a glass of something strong in one hand and the remote control in the other.

The first step is simply to awaken to the fact that you might be addicted to TV or (at best) seduced by its nightly thrall. Once you've noticed or admitted this, you'll find yourself in a stronger position to step back and observe how you feel after watching it for long periods: almost certainly dulled, tetchy, irritable and de-energized.

Try a week without TV (why do you recoil from that suggestion if you're not addicted?), and you may well notice some striking things: first, that (at the start of the week) you are itching to put it on; next, that you wonder what you will do without it. (It's a big space to fill.) You might then notice the creativity that begins to flow simply from looking for something else to do, whether it's reading, tidying, praying, talking, walking, journalling, or even simply stopping to slow down and 'be' yourself (when did you last do that?). You may also notice that you begin to 'overhear' yourself, perhaps for the first time in a while – now that the cacophony of soap characters, advertisers and reality contestants has been silenced. And you may just find that you begin to look forward to your evenings, and discover an energy that you thought you'd mislaid long ago. This is, indeed, a form of awakening from spiritual sleep.

* * *

What do we do when the power fails?

One of my favourite authors is Douglas Coupland, the man who wrote the best-selling novel *Generation X*. In a lovely little book called *Polaroids from the Dead*, he asks a brilliant question: What do we do when the power fails?

It's a strangely beautiful thing when the power fails. We reach for the candles, and suddenly the atmosphere changes. Coupland observes that we sing songs, tell each other stories, rediscover something of our connectedness and humanity. When the power comes back on, we atomize once more.

One of my happiest memories of married life is a short camping trip we made to a forest in France; it was dark at night, pitch dark, and quiet, and we ended up playing Scrabble on a camping table in the open air till the early hours. We became present, somehow, to each other and to the world around us in a way we had previously not experienced, as we sat there quietly and enjoyed the stillness of each other's company. So why don't we do that when we get home?

Sometimes it takes a power failure to remind us of what lies beyond the background noise and distraction. Coupland concludes, 'I want to live my life in a permanent state of power failure.' When I saw those words for the first time, a switch flicked (off) in my mind.

* * *

We have to start somewhere, and TV is a good place to start because so many of us are trapped by it, and we offer it so much of our time. It is also symbolic of the culture that can seduce and distract us from the art of living – it is visual, fragmented, consumerist and desensitizing. TV culture creates an alternative form of reality for us; it replaces our imagination with a script written by those who want you to fall asleep and dream of what they'd love to sell you.

But what else do you need to awaken from? Only you will truly know. If you have a rigid daily routine, perhaps you'll find that you are cruising on autopilot, or stuck in a rut. You may need to become aware of that and awaken from the sleepwalk. Remember, awareness is the start of awakening.

Perhaps, at work, you find yourself spending more time escaping into the Internet than you should – not maliciously wasting time, but because you can't face doing what needs to be done, or because you're just putting life off in general. Some days you might return home feeling that you've done little else but 'kill time'. It's time to awaken from that pattern.

You may need to awaken from the slumber of other behavioural patterns, which you have grown so used to that you could do them in your sleep. Have you noticed how you react to people if they challenge you or frustrate you? Have you spotted how judgmental you have become? Have you observed how you're always so willing to help others that you have no time for yourself? Or how you're so obsessed with yourself that you have no time for others?

Something might have even 'shut you down' – a failed relationship may have triggered a fear of being rejected that keeps you from being truly open with others, for example; a fearsome teacher may have stifled your willingness to take a risk because you were afraid to make mistakes in front of them… The good news is that you can awaken from the patterns of behaviour you have fallen into, the patterns you resort to by default. Some may be positive; others less so. But you don't have to worry about 'fixing' them, for now, or even judging them. All you need to do is stop to notice things; that is the start you need.

* * *

How do we awaken? Two exercises ...

The lifeline: 360-degree reflection

One way of awakening to who you are and how you've ended up here is to seek feedback from people you trust. You may wish to ask a cross section of people from different strands of your life – people who know you well, and whom you trust – to offer you some sensitive comment on the state you're in. This is not a chance for them to try to change you; rather, it is an opportunity for you to awaken to how others see you and to learn something of yourself from their perspective. Some feedback may challenge you, but if it is offered as a gift, it should also awaken you gently to the place in which you may now find yourself. For now, receive this. Don't wrestle with it, argue with it or seek to change anything. Just rediscover who you might really be.

A life in the day – pattern recognition

Another way of awakening to your present reality is to observe yourself for one day, and to look upon that day as a microcosm of the rest of your life.

Try to take a reasonably typical weekday, and note down what you do, who you're with, how you feel at different points, and how you react to your various circumstances.

Once you have done this, 'step back' and look at this day as if it were a representation of the way you construct the whole of your life. There may be exceptional circumstances that are not typical of the norm – if so, disregard those for now. Instead, focus on compiling an honest picture of a typical day.

Try to observe things that form a pattern: How do you start your day? If you work, how long does it take you to get there? How do you spend the 'dead' travelling time? What are your mornings comprised of? How do the people you spend time with affect you? How do you affect them? What is your lunchtime routine? Do you take exercise? Do you cook your own food in the evening or have a ready-meal or take away? How do you feel as you approach your evening? How much do you drink? How do you feel when you are going to sleep? Are you anxious or stressed? Are you at peace?

How much money have you spent, and on what? How much TV have you watched? How much time have you spent away from the background noise of mp3 players or car radios or CD players or lift muzak? How much time have you spent in prayer, or reflection? Have you encouraged others? Have you generated any random acts of kindness, or secret moments of generosity? How much have you received from people (emotionally, physically, spiritually...) and how much have you given? How much have you talked and how much have you listened?

Now, of course no day is ever the same. But in observing the rhythm and shape of a fairly typical day, you might spot recurring themes. For instance, you might realize that you're typically getting through half a bottle of wine a night, which equals roughly £3 ($4.40) – and adds up to £21 ($30) a week or £90 ($130) a month... And, more importantly, it might (depending on how you 'use' alcohol) mean that you are indulging in a nightly act of escape – from the pressures of your day, or your fears for tomorrow – which adds up to a lot of time spent on the run.

Positively, you might see that taking a few moments every day to speak to the security man on the door at your place of work, or to the parents at the school gate, adds up to a pattern of investment in other people – who may often feel invisible and forgotten – that will yield long-term positive results both for you and for them.

Think or pray about what you observe, and ask those who are closest to you – and are intrinsically part of your day – to reflect as well. Are there any patterns you would like to break? Are there any you would like to affirm? How do the smallest, seemingly insignificant parts of your day accumulate over time into something more substantial?

* * *

What wakes you up?

Moments of awakening usually come to us as a gift. Frequently, they arise when we manage to stop talking or even thinking and start listening instead. And very often, they come to us quietly, almost insignificantly. These are the times to really listen up. The Bible certainly contains stories of angels singing in the sky and even supernatural 'writing on the wall' (for King Nebuchadnezzar), but an awakening is more likely to come as it did to the prophet Elijah – in a 'still, small voice'.

The Bible tells that 'a hurricane wind ripped through the mountains and shattered the rocks before God, but God wasn't to be found in the wind; after the wind came an earthquake, but God wasn't in the earthquake; and after the earthquake fire, but God wasn't in the fire; and after the fire a gentle and quiet whisper.' And the gentle, quiet whisper spoke to Elijah; it was the voice of God.

It's hard to become aware of anything around you if you are perpetually distracted; it's hard to listen for the still, small voice or the 'gentle, quiet whisper' if you are talking all the time or looking only for angels in the sky.

We can be awakened by many things; from direct interventions from God that come out of the blue, to the simplicity of a flower in bloom which we'd normally just walk by, we can learn from each moment of clarity or 'epiphany'. Sometimes, all it takes is the effort of stopping to notice something we wouldn't normally look twice at – the homeless person we walk past on the street, perhaps, or the colour of your friend's eyes – something that can help us awaken to the world around us, or even to ourselves.

So whether it's the death of a loved one, a sudden illness, the loss of something we hold dear, something challenging we read, a snippet of conversation we overhear, a song lyric, a direct epiphany, a holiday, a moment of success at work... be on the lookout. John Eldredge writes in his book *The Journey of Desire* about a friend of his who observed a sunset and was prepared to be moved by the experience:

> *'We have had a couple of inspiring sunsets this week,' a dear friend wrote in an e-mail. 'It was as if the seams of our atmosphere split for a bit of heaven to plunge into the sea. I stood and applauded...*

> *simultaneously I wanted to kneel and weep.*
> *We can be shocked into awakening from a slumber, like a bucket of*
> *cold water that has been thrown over our heads. Other awakenings*
> *are more gradual, less spectacular. But almost always, if we are*
> *observant, we'll notice that something resonates with our spirit. There*
> *will be a moment when it feels like time stands still; when the hairs*
> *on the back of our neck stand on end. And in those moments, it is as if*
> *something or someone is speaking to us.*[2]

Clearing ground

People who are spiritually mature create daily rhythms to allow them to listen actively. Spend time with someone who is spiritually wise and you'll notice that they are rarely (if ever) tightly strung or trying to force an agenda. And this is the spirit to carry into your own time of reflection. Most of us only indulge in times of quiet or retreat in order to seek direction in our lives, as to which way we should go or which path we should choose. A career change, a house move, a financial decision, and so on. Yet often the most profound awakenings arise from being willing to let go of the 'Where now?' or 'What next?' questions. In fact, most of us need to let go profoundly before we take anything more on.

So 'clearing a space' in our lives has to work on at least two levels. We must clear space in order to hear the still, small voice speak to us. But we must also be prepared, within that act of space-clearing, for yet more clearing to take place – to discern what we first need to surrender before we can move on with a lighter load. The poet, priest and mystic John O'Donohue once wrote that we must 'clear thickets in the undergrowth of banality in our life' so that we can overhear our true self. We should first clear space in order to ask, 'What more should I clear?'

Just as we must hold lightly to any agenda as we clear thickets in our life, so we must also be careful not to 'attach' ourselves too strongly to anything we experience within the space that opens up. For we can end up trying to possess that which is not ours; or we can worship the experience itself and become fixated on the voice, instead of what it says.

* * *

Stop to think

Stop to think for a few moments: when did you last sense an awakening? It may have been this month. It may not have been for years. What happened? How did it arise within you? Who or what was the catalyst? How did it make you feel?

Did you act on this awakening? If so, what happened?

If not, what might have happened? How might your life have been different if you had?

* * *

It's one thing to experience an awakening. As we considered at the very start of the chapter, it's another thing to spring out of bed and seize the day. If we are not to press snooze and slip back under the covers, it's crucial that we mark such moments and then act upon them – or let them act upon us, more to the point. And so we must, if you like, begin to travel the journey of our four icons, making the transition from experiencing an awakening into seeing the world in a brand new way, with fresh eyes. The kind of eyes that perhaps need to blink a few times and focus to adjust to the sun-filled morning after the darkness of a very long night.

Chapter 2

Seeing afresh

*Faith is to believe what you do not yet see; the reward for this
faith is to see what you believe.*
St Augustine

St Augustine made this suggestion 1,600 years ago. 'Open your
eyes,' he seems to be saying. 'You don't have to be a Zen master
to sense that things are not always as they *appear* in this world.'
There is more to life than we usually spot with our ordinary
eyes.

The writer of the biblical book of Ecclesiastes suggests that God
'has set eternity in the hearts of [people]' (Ecclesiastes 3:11). It's
an intriguing, unsettling, beautiful verse. Deep down, something
whispers to every single one of us that life could and should be
more *epic*; as we watch the great films or read the classic books or
listen to the spine-tingling tunes that provide the soundtrack to
our lives, we can't help but notice something tugging at our hearts.
It's what John O'Donohue called 'overhearing yourself'.

Deep tries to call to deep, from all sorts of different places, and it
keeps on calling. It refuses to give up. Every time we lay our head
on the pillow, every time we experience a birth or a death, every
time we discover some treasure buried within the ordinariness of
our lives, every time we look at the stars, it's easy enough to see
that there is a lot more to our inner lives than we would often be
willing to admit.

The trouble is, we can't always *see* our own life unfolding like the
epic plot we yearn for it to be. So often, our busyness or tedious
routines tell a different story: it's not working out the way we'd
planned; we're not the person we dreamed of becoming; we've
become bored or distracted or unfulfilled... and we cannot, for

the life of us, see ourselves as adventurers, pioneers, heroes or brave hearts in a brave new world.

The gap between our heartfelt longing and the reality of our sometimes humdrum existence can seem insurmountable to many of us, and we can end up feeling stranded, frustrated, and sometimes in despair.

For others, the gap can be an inspiration. It depends on how you see things.

And that's where St Augustine's faith comes in. Faith is about believing when you cannot see. It begins to move you from one place to another – from the place where you accept the status quo, to... Whatever it looks like, the reward is to see what you believe. The songwriter Bono put it a different way in U2's beautiful song 'Walk On': 'We're packing a suitcase for a place none of us has been; a place that has to be believed to be seen.'

Believing and seeing; it's part of the same, spiritually intelligent package: it's about seeing life with a fresh set of eyes; about staring long and hard and deep into the state of your being, our being, and beginning to see how things really can be different.

The great writers, theologians, poets, musicians and artists are like cultural 'seers'; they sense and see the world in a different way, and challenge us to look creatively through their eyes at what – or more crucially *how* – they see. They help to bridge the gap between our existential longing and the reality in which we find ourselves.

But they cannot, ultimately, do the seeing for us, of course. 'Seeing afresh' is no passive acceptance of someone else's perspective. It is a journey of discovery, and we all have the wherewithal within us to begin that journey. As Bono said, it's about packing a suitcase – setting out, going after what you have glimpsed as an awakening in your heart.

Some of the best journeys we make are the ones in which we can't see where we're going – we just know we have to set off. They can be scary, exhilarating, demanding, fulfilling. But one thing is for certain: you feel alive when you're on them. At such times, we have to believe that we will reach somewhere different in the end. (Sometimes we come back to where we started, but end up with a very different way of seeing that same place.) It's only when we make a start, in faith, that we begin to see with fresh eyes where the journey might lead us. And it's only then that we begin to see that the journey itself is more significant than the destination – and that the *way* we travel will determine where we finally end up.

As Marcel Proust wrote, 'The real voyage of discovery consists not in seeking new lands but in seeing with new eyes.' It's as we begin to see the possibilities of a life lived in a new way that our journey takes a new direction – hopefully, one for the better.

* * *

How do you see the world?

Consider the human iris. No iris is the same – not even identical twins share the same pattern. That's why security technology has been developed (in our fear-driven world) to read and record our iris as a unique identifying mark, as we pass through passport control, for example.

And now consider this: according to the Jewish tradition, we are 'fearfully and wonderfully made'. Those words are found in a psalm (Psalm 139) that tells poetically of how God wove us together in our mother's womb; he knows the number of hairs on our heads and the number of days in our lives. Yet we are all unique. No one laughs quite like you, looks quite like you, loves quite like you. The psalm says we each reflect uniquely something of the image of the invisible God. What a thought.

And as such, we see the world in our own way. No one sees it quite the way I do; no one sees it quite the way you do. That's a truly amazing thing. And therefore, the way you see the world matters.

* * *

Stop to look
Look up from your book for a few moments.
   What do you see?
   How do you see?
   What are you hoping to see?
   What are you looking *for*?

* * *

Now, stop to think
What is unique about the way you see the world? What have people said to you about your own insight? If someone asked you to share your vision, what would it be? What details do you think you notice that no one else sees? What do you love to show others?

How have you helped others to see the world in a fresh light? Think of one occasion when you changed the way someone around you saw their world.

* * *

Ultimately, we must ask ourselves how we *respond* to the way we see the world – and that's where we're heading with our next icon, as we consider how we react creatively to seeing the world afresh. But first we must gain fresh perspective. In fact, unless we stop – to look, and look again, and wonder, and reflect – then there is no point in us rushing to action whatsoever. As someone once said, 'Don't just do something, stand there!'

* * *

'Leisure'

What is this life if, full of care,
We have no time to stand and stare.

No time to stand beneath the boughs
And stare as long as sheep or cows.

No time to see, when woods we pass,
Where squirrels hide their nuts in grass.

No time to see, in broad daylight,
Streams full of stars, like skies at night.

No time to turn at Beauty's glance,
And watch her feet, how they can dance.

*No time to wait till her mouth can
Enrich that smile her eyes began.*

*A poor life this if, full of care,
We have no time to stand and stare.*
William Henry Davies

* * *

Watching the world go by

One of the greatest temptations, in our image-saturated culture, is to become *voyeurs* – consuming passively the images that flash before us in a disconnected, never-ending flood of visual shards and fragments. We are awash with so many images – from billboards to glossy magazines to TV screens to websites to mobile phones – that our eyes can glaze over fast. One moment we can be watching a programme about drought; in the blink of an eye, an advert for sparkling mineral water appears... We skim the visual surface of the world before us, amid the flotsam and jetsam that drifts on a tide of consumer culture.

If you are spiritually intelligent, you will be careful what you look at. The most obvious example is pornography (though there are many others). You may be able to delete images from a computer screen, but it's a different matter trying to erase the hard drive of your mind. We have probably all seen things we wish we hadn't seen.

But overly religious people aren't always the most spiritually intelligent. They tend to fixate on not watching this or that because it's sexually immoral or violent or unhelpful – at the cost of asking *how* they engage with the world. It's one thing to keep your mind clean by averting your eyes when something unhelpful appears on the TV; it's quite another to use your eyes creatively and perceptively to see what's really going on around you.

* * *

Stop to think
Sometimes if you're talking to someone, you'll get the distinct impression that they're not fully 'with' you – the lights are on, as

we say, but there's no one home. Their eyes have glazed over. They are dulled to the world around them. Others watch carefully, look closely, keep their eyes peeled. You can tell the people who seem most alive, as they usually have a glint in their eye.

What do people see when they look in your eyes?

* * *

Keep watch!

We thought in the last chapter about awakening from the sleepwalk of life. There's a very close correlation between being wakeful and being watchful. As the Buddha says in the *Dhammapada*:

> *Wakefulness is the way to life.*
> *The fool sleeps*
> *As if he were already dead,*
> *But the Master is awake*
> *And he lives forever.*
>
> *He watches.*
> *He is clear.*
>
> *How happy he is!*
> *For he sees that wakefulness is life.*
> *How happy he is,*
> *Following the path of the awakened.*

Become aware of what is happening around you. Even right now. What can you hear? How do you feel? Are you tense? Have you remembered to breathe? Notice things. Spot the small details. See who is struggling or left out of things. Watch for the changing of the seasons. Observe how your routine and rhythm make you feel. Keep looking with curiosity at the way life is unfolding before you. You don't want to miss your cue...

* * *

Familiarity breeds contempt

Have you ever caught yourself looking at something terribly familiar, like the pens on your desk or the clock on the wall or the colour of your car or the contours of your partner or the shape of your colleague's nose, and thought, 'I've never actually noticed that before...'?

Just occasionally we get a fresh, almost other-worldly glimpse, as though we are seeing our own familiar situation from a stranger's perspective. These are great moments, when we are offered the chance of seeing afresh. They are gifts, which stop us in our tracks, albeit for a moment; within them, we might notice something about the room we're in, or the person we've lived with for many, many years – something we've never noticed before. However, such moments are so rare that we hardly ever act upon them. They pass in a moment; they might cause us to shiver, to frown, to smile – but how do we embrace that moment, make the most of it, use it to transform us?

I like running, and I try to run every day, if I can. There are any number of potentially inspiring routes from my house into the countryside: lanes and bridleways, pathways and fields. When we moved to the area, everything seemed fresh, new, vivid. Yet soon, I settled into a familiar running routine and I have found it hard to break out and try a different path.

Almost invariably, if I ever do run off the beaten track, I am rewarded with a fresh view, a surprise of some kind, a new take on familiar territory. So why am I so reluctant to try this more often?

Perhaps you are similar. Perhaps you have the same old commuter routine worked out to a tee – the precise time to arrive at the station, where to stand on the platform, which route to take at the other end. Of course, you can't always break free from the norm – but if you were at least to walk a different route once a week, or sit on a different carriage for a day, then you might see something different, and you might see something differently.

* * *

Stop to think
We can perform any number of *small acts of subversion* to break

33

our usual line of sight. What you have seen differently, lately? Your partner? Your job? Your faith? Your self?

* * *

Start to act
The next time you walk a familiar path, look up, look down, and try to see the people and buildings and trees and signs afresh. Notice colours. Notice words. Notice people, and their expressions. Notice how fast you are walking. Notice that your mind is probably racing ahead of you even faster, thinking of who you're about to meet or what you're about to do. Try instead, even for a moment, simply to enjoy the journey. Walk a little slower. Relax your shoulders. And focus on the travelling, not the arrival. Ask yourself what you begin to notice.

* * *

If you stop to notice, you will start to notice

This is an excerpt from Jon McGregor's beautiful novel, *If Nobody Speaks of Remarkable Things*. It notices the things we normally fail to see; the rhythms and sounds and sights and smells around us that might otherwise go unnoticed, unspoken, uncelebrated, undiscovered.

If you listen, you can hear it. The city, it sings. If you stand quietly, at the foot of a garden, in the middle of a street, on the roof of a house. It's clearest at night, when the sound cuts more sharply across the surface of things, when the song reaches out to a place inside you. It's a wordless song, for the most, but it's a song all the same, and nobody hearing it could doubt what it sings. And the song sings the loudest when you pick out each note. The low soothing hum of air-conditioners, fanning out the heat and the smells of shops and cafes and offices across the city, winding up and winding down, long breaths layered upon each other, a lullaby hum for tired streets. The rush of traffic still cutting across flyovers, even in the dark hours a constant rush of sound, tyres rolling across tarmac and engines rumbling, loose drains and

> *manhole covers clack-clacking like cast-iron castanets... And*
> *all the alarms, calling for help, each district and quarter, each*
> *street and estate, each every way you turn has alarms going off,*
> *coming on, going off, coming on, a hammered ring like a lightning*
> *drum-roll, like a mesmeric bell-toll, the false and the real as loud*
> *as each other, crying their needs to the night like an understaffed*
> *orphanage, babies waawaa-ing in darkened wards.*[1]

McGregor finds sacredness within the mundane. So often, we miss what is sacred around us, that which is 'remarkable', because we are looking instead for the sensational – for the stand-out moments, for the drop-dead gorgeous people, for the cool-as experiences. The remarkable is all around us: but we usually don't see it, because we don't know how to look for it. If you stop to notice, you will start to notice: a voice rising from outside your window, a bird singing above the traffic noise, the shape of the clouds, the quality of light... And you, you are part of this landscape: a remarkable character within the unfolding story of this time and this place.

* * *

In the film *Dead Poets Society*, Robin Williams's character, Mr Keating, provides an inspirational figure for the boys he teaches, and for the millions who watched the film. In an iconic moment, Keating climbs onto his desk, to the bemusement of his pupils, and begins to speak:

'Why do I stand up here? Anybody...? [...] I stand upon my desk to remind myself that we must constantly look at things in a different way. You see, the world looks very different from up here. You don't believe me? Come see for yourself. Come on. Come on!'

The boys begin to stand on his desk. Keating jumps down. 'Just when you think you know something, you have to look at it in another way. Even though it may seem silly or wrong, you must try! ... Thoreau said, "Most men lead lives of quiet desperation." Don't be resigned to that. Break out!'

* * *

As well as standing taller, like Mr Keating, we also have the option to fall to our knees. From down there, the world, again, looks different. Every now and again, I remember that my little boy and girl see the world quite literally from a different perspective. So I get down on my knees and look up at the giant table and chairs, the ceiling that seems so far away, the door handles that are out of reach, and I wonder what it is like to be like a little child once more.

The world looks so different to children. Life looks different. Sometimes we need to get on our knees to see the world God has made for us. It's there all around us, but perhaps we've forgotten just how lovely it can look.

The good news is we don't have to. We are going on a journey, packing a suitcase for a place that has to be believed to be seen.

Moving.

Chapter 3

Living the change

A farmer went out to sow. And as he sowed, some seeds fell on the path, and the birds came and ate them up. Other seeds fell on rocky ground, where they did not have much soil, and they sprang up quickly, since they had no depth of soil. But when the sun rose, they were scorched; and since they had no root, they withered away. Other seeds fell among thorns, and the thorns grew up and choked them. Other seeds fell on good soil and brought forth grain, some a hundredfold, some sixty, some thirty.
Matthew 13:3–8

It's one thing to awaken to a deeper reality, and to begin to see the world around you from a fresh perspective. But unless you respond creatively and lastingly, you will remain locked in a world of ideas, however beautiful they may be. Spirituality is about maintaining the tension between contemplation (being) and action (doing). It bridges the two, although the movement from contemplation to action is never one-way. It should be a perpetual two-way flow, one constantly enriching the other.

Jesus was unnervingly realistic about the challenge facing anyone who wants to enter what he calls 'the kingdom' – life as God intended it. He knew that many people would hear his words, but not everyone would respond. In fact, in the parable of the sower, only one of the four categories of listener truly yields fruit. That's not a high ratio.

Sadly, many 'Mind, Body and Spirit' gurus and religious leaders promise a consumerist quick fix: instant enlightenment for anyone who fancies a dash of spiritual lifestyle cool, if you like. And likewise, many people approach spirituality as 'consumers', as if it were something that should serve them, instead of something to serve.

But it isn't about just reading the book and getting the T-shirt. It takes resolve to move from thinking about transformation to living it out. How many of us keep promising that 'soon' we'll go on a diet or quit smoking or start spending more time with our families or do something truly life-changing or...? It's one thing knowing that we should; it's another putting it into action.

And that's why the spiritual path is far from being a 'soft' option for anyone: it calls for courage, the courage of your convictions, and commitment. It may be a simple path to walk, but it's not always an easy one. You know you've experienced moments of awakening. You've begun to understand what's going on... The question now is: *What are you going to do about it?*

* * *

Stop to think
Here's how Jesus explained the different types of soil in his parable. Which type are you – 1, 2, 3 or 4?

1. If you don't understand the message about the kingdom of God, it's as though the seed falls on the path and is eaten by birds.

2. The rocky soil is like the person who hears and receives the message with joy, but the seeds cannot take root and so wither when the first challenges come.

3. The thorny ground represents 'the worries of this life' and 'the deceitfulness of wealth', which choke the growth of the seed.

4. The good soil represents the one who hears and understands, and who 'produces a crop...'

* * *

Changes

Remember Mr Keating's words from *Dead Poets Society* in the last chapter: 'Thoreau said, "Most men lead lives of quiet desperation." Don't be resigned to that. Break out!'

Once Keating had climbed down from his desk and shown his pupils that you don't have to see the world in the same old, same old way, he didn't just dismiss the class. He set them the task of writing a poem.

It can sometimes seem daunting to work out how you respond creatively to a fresh insight, especially if that insight is profoundly challenging. But respond you must: otherwise, the seeds of awakening will fall on stony or thorny ground and be eaten by birds or choked by thistles. It is crucial to act, even if the first, simple act you take is symbolic or very small. It shows you that it can be done. It puts a stake in the ground. And it demonstrates that a small act of change can be the most liberating thing you've ever done. As Gandhi once said, we must 'be the change we wish to see' in the world.

Change one thing!

Every New Year's Eve, most of us think about 'resolutions' – things we plan to change about ourselves, given the opportunity for a fresh start on 1 January. Something in us responds to the challenge of wiping the slate clean and starting again. It somehow seems appealing.

And yet, how many of us manage to turn a resolution into sustained, sustainable action? By mid-January, we've stopped going to the gym or started snacking again (or whatever the resolution is) and it can be disheartening to feel as if we can't make the change we know we'd like to.

A well-known chemist chain in the UK ran an intriguing marketing campaign one year with the strapline, 'Change One Thing!' Its website at the time advised, 'Most of us lose motivation, and usually for the same reasons: We aim too high, don't have enough support and don't plan or prepare properly.' And they were probably right.

When it comes to embarking on a spiritual journey towards becoming more fully human, it's tempting to dream 'big', and it's good to want to change the world. But none of us can change the world single-handedly; and change will only come about when we begin to demonstrate the positive benefits in our own lives. So we need to change our own world first. How much better to start small – and change *something* – than to dream so big that you change nothing?

Malcolm Gladwell, who wrote the best-selling book *The Tipping Point*, talks about the power of making small changes in our own lives (which can lead, very quickly, to big changes in society). 'The virtue of an epidemic, after all, is that just a little input is enough to get it started, and it can spread very quickly,' he writes.

Gladwell uses a delightful analogy of rain turning to snow. Just occasionally, we can be taken by surprise when a constant, ugly drizzle suddenly turns white and we have a snow storm to enjoy. The conditions, of course, have to be just right.

'Almost nothing had changed,' he recalls of one such occurrence, 'and yet – and this was the amazing thing – everything had changed. Rain had become something entirely different: snow! We are all, at heart, gradualists, our expectations set by the steady passage of time. But the world of the tipping point is a place where the unexpected becomes expected, where radical change is more than a possibility. It is contrary to all our expectations – a certainty.'[1]

On our spiritual journey, we arrive at a point of departure. The awakenings we receive begin to add up; the conditions become favourable and one small change can make a big difference. Rain can turn to snow. If you have arrived at a point of spiritual departure, it's as if the temperature outside is 1°C (34°F) and beginning to drop.

* * *

Stop to think

Reflect upon the new ways of seeing, and the awakenings you have experienced, which we discussed in the first two chapters. They are likely to have provoked a reaction within you, deep down, a desire to change one thing. It might be specific; it might be more general. But now, consider what one, small but sustainable change in your life might help to change your rain to snow.

* * *

Where are you headed?

If you consider 'change' as an element of your own journey, then the coaching guru John Whitmore's words make some mysterious sense here. 'If we do not change direction,' he suggests, 'we are likely to end up where we are heading.' Where are you heading if you do not change direction? Just as it only takes a one-degree change in temperature to change the weather, so it only takes the slightest pressure on a rudder to change the direction of a ship.

* * *

Bearing small fruits

A former colleague of mine, Mark Greene, director of the London Institute for Contemporary Christianity, has a lovely term for small-scale change which can make a big difference both to you and the world around you. He calls it 'small fruits'. It's a way, perhaps, of taking stock and taking encouragement along your journey, of seeing what difference your journey is making.

But what kind of fruit do you wish to be growing? It's important to reflect, as not every 'change' you make will necessarily or automatically be positive. The spiritual searcher who decides that they need to retreat from the everyday realities of this world risks becoming marooned from real 'life' – so we need constantly to ask whether the awakenings and fresh perspectives we are gaining are translating into positive outcomes for everyday living. The person who ends up spending all their time contemplating, for example, may end up retreating from significant relationships; whereas the act of contemplation – the being – should be kept in tension with the doing, and should therefore refresh and revitalize your relationships positively.

Fruit can grow in many forms: love, joy, peace, patience, kindness, goodness, faithfulness, gentleness, self-control... If you make a change that yields such 'fruit', you are on course to change the way you were once headed.

Small fruits create wide-scale change

Remember Gladwell's words about creating an epidemic with little effort: 'The virtue of an epidemic... is that just a little input is enough to get it started, and it can spread very quickly.' My former colleague Mark used to walk past a telephone box on his way to work in London that was filled with prostitutes' calling cards. They all contained images that were unsuitable to be displayed in public places; none of us would like our children to see them. He wondered what he could do to stem this particular tide, and felt helpless. London contains hundreds of these phone boxes, and the actions of one man would surely not be enough to clean up the streets.

But he knew he had to do something if he were to live by the courage of his convictions. So he adopted this one box, and every morning when he came into work, he removed all the cards. By the evening, the box was full again, so he would also remove them again on his way home. News began to spread about his actions, especially when he was attacked by a 'tom carder', the person responsible for putting them up. In the end, *The Independent* newspaper reported on his actions, and Westminster City Council supported the enterprise. As the *Independent* reported, 'Westminster councillor Kit Malthouse said: "If people-power goes out there to clear them [phone boxes] it will shame the Government into doing something about it."'

We can all feel frustrated at not being able to change the world; but if we admit that we can't, and instead seek to link arms with those around us, each by focusing on one small change, then together we may just be able to reach around the world.

* * *

Change can only ever happen in the present (so stop wishing you could change the past or the future!)

It's the simplest idea, but perhaps one of the most profound, and one of the hardest to grasp: you can't bring about change in the past or the future, but only the present. We will consider in greater detail the art of becoming more fully 'present to the present' in following chapters, as this is such an important part of becoming more 'spiritually intelligent'. But for now, consider this: how much time do you spend (and waste) wishing you could change the things you have done in the past, or longing for change to come at a future date, when (for example) you may get a new job, or win the lottery, or meet someone special, or start really living life the way you'd like to live it?

Most of us fail to grasp what it means to live in the present, but we can begin to change that by making change happen *now*. The man who promises himself he'll stop smoking tomorrow will perpetually live in a state of denial. For tomorrow, of course, never comes. The woman who wishes she could turn back time and turn left instead of right at a crossroads in her life also lives in a state of perpetual denial, because unlike the British cult sci-fi hero Doctor Who, we have not learned to travel through time.

Instead, we can only do something about our lives in the here and now. We have to act upon our awakenings today; otherwise they will never take root.

* * *

Start to act
We thought earlier in this chapter about one thing you would like to change, having reflected on the way you are beginning to see the world afresh. Now, don't just resolve to make this small change happen: begin right now. Try to make the change today. Go and do it now.

* * *

Tools to help you

While 'writing a diary' might be something you stopped at school, the art of writing a journal can help to bridge the gap between contemplation and action. First, it helps you to remember the moments of awakening you have experienced, and the new way in which you are seeing the world. Second, it helps you to think those moments through more fully and creatively. Third, it offers you the chance to challenge yourself and hold yourself accountable.

Beginning a journal is an example of effecting a small change. Admittedly, it is about reflecting. But it is nevertheless an action, and one that takes little effort, if you try to write a little every day (or every week). A journal will soon give you a sense of where you've come from, and will help you to record how you have responded creatively and decisively to your spiritual awakening.

Prayer or quiet time alone is another example of something you can do daily, which will soon begin to yield positive results. If you have never stopped simply to be quiet, to listen, to 'be', then you probably need to start. But don't try to become a Zen guru overnight. Instead, why not try stopping for 5 minutes at your desk in the morning before you switch on your computer, to still yourself and to prepare spiritually for the coming day.

In Chapter 1, I suggested an exercise to try called 'A life in the day', in which you consider how the smallest of actions, if repeated every day, help to determine your 'way' of life. You might like to revisit that exercise now, and consider one extra action that will, over time, help to change both the direction of your life and (more importantly) the way you get there. It may simply be that you decide to smile at the bus driver and say hello. These tiny actions will build up, and have a positive, accumulative effect, not just on you but on those around you.

* * *

Ultimately, you will not become more spiritually intelligent simply by doing a load of new things and trying to prove to yourself that you are different. But in trying to act upon one small area that you have glimpsed through awakening to a new possibility, you will start to move yourself and others into a new space. The goal is to live actively, not passively: taking good decisions, serving others in selfless love, and making the difference you know, deep down, you would love to make. Life is about being and doing. And it is about growing – growing up and into the person you were created to be. You don't always notice that you have changed overnight: if you are losing weight, for example, you won't notice the change immediately. But if you resolve to stop snacking today, and to start walking to work instead of driving, for instance, there will come a time before long when someone says to you, 'Wow, you look different – what's happened?' It's at that point that your rain will turn to snow.

Chapter 4

Passing it on

Love spreads.
The Stone Roses

And so, we reach the end of the first leg of the journey. We have looked for fresh awakenings, sought to see the world through fresh eyes, and asked how we begin to live the change we'd like to see. The final step involves 'passing on' what we have experienced.

But let's be clear right from the very start: this icon, the arrow, does not involve trying to change other people. Neither does it imply the need to 'convert' them spiritually to your way of thinking. In fact, quite the reverse is true.

It is about sharing the excitement of your own unfolding journey, and passing on the benefits of the change you have experienced to others – the benefits of becoming more fully present, more curious and aware, more compassionate and more servant-minded towards those around you. It's about leaving your preconceptions and prejudices behind, suspending judgment of others, seeing past their identikit props to who they really are, receiving life as a gift and sharing the treasure of your own unfolding with others.

Why pass on anything?

Life in the twenty-first century is not without its challenges. We know the score by now: there is global poverty and huge inequality. Climate change hangs over us like a dark cloud of smog. And even though we, in the West, have indescribably more material wealth than most of the rest of the world, we suffer from depression, addiction, fear of terrorism, economic instability and an apathy that paralyzes us, as if we've forgotten why we're here and where we're meant to be going.

This is no longer the time (as if it were ever the time) for the 'me-first' attitude that has become so prevalent in our culture of rampant consumerism. It is not the time to pull up the drawbridge and cut ourselves off from those who are different, or who are poor, or who are opposed to our way of life. It is not the time to hoard what we have for ourselves, but instead to orient ourselves in the direction of generous living. The good life (so often interpreted selfishly to mean the comfortable life) must now be replaced by the generous life if we are to rise to the enormous challenges that face us in today's world, both as individuals and as a society.

The generous life implies sharing, but it's not just about sharing material riches. If we are truly to live generously then we must take the opportunity to share any good news that we awaken to, about how life really can be lived in our fast-forward, frenzied and frenetic culture. As we tap into our innate spiritual intelligence, sharing will become a way of life: sharing wisdom for the journey, sharing stories, sharing life. Passing on the benefits, if you like.

As mentioned, it's not about trying to change other people, but exemplifying a positive transformation in me. If my world is beginning to change for the better, then I will begin to make the world around me better for those who come into my orbit. I will welcome them instead of shun them; I will embrace them instead of ignore them. I will become hospitable, arms outstretched, and share the riches of life I begin to gain.

* * *

What's wrong with you?

Sadly, one of the easiest things in the world for us to do is to see what's wrong with others. You can take any person you know and find fault with them (well, almost anyone). And their shortcomings usually come into the sharpest relief when they do something wrong to *you*: forget your birthday, rub you up the wrong way, cut you up on the road…

But we should not focus on the 'speck of dust' in someone else's eye when we have 'a plank' in our own, as the saying goes. For while we are focused on other people, it's dangerously easy to neglect who *we* are becoming.

Let's think about that some more before we move on. The Bible story goes that a woman was caught in adultery, and the religious authorities took her to Jesus, trying to trap him. The law, they said, demanded that she be stoned. 'What do *you* say?' they asked.

Jesus took what must have seemed to the woman like a lifetime to answer their question. He drew a line in the sand. 'Let anyone among you who is without sin be the first to throw a stone at her,' he finally suggested.[1] I'm sure you could have heard a pin drop, as well as a few stones.

His reply turns everything on its head. This story is not about the woman after all, but about our own reaction to her, or people like her. It takes her out of the spotlight and puts us, those who are looking on, firmly into it. Gradually, the crowd melts away, understanding that they are not in a position to cast stones at others when they are worthy of judgment themselves.

How do we react when we hear about a paedophile being convicted, or if we see someone acting antisocially in the street, or generally doing something we believe we wouldn't – couldn't – do? Certainly, the easiest thing to do is to judge them; it makes us feel better about ourselves. For all the while someone else is in the wrong, we can stay in the right.

Such an attitude translates to the way we view other people, full-stop. If we ever watch Jerry-Springer-style daytime TV 'talk' shows – often involving poor families who have experienced a breakdown in relationships – we most probably do so, sub-consciously, to feel better about ourselves. Thank God we're not like them, we almost certainly think.

In fact, it's hard not to walk down the street, even, in the posture of judgment – scrutinizing people's fashion sense, their attractiveness, their social position or class, how their children behave, and so on – and not compare them with ourselves. But 'judge not, lest you be judged,' said Jesus. Worry about yourself and what you need to do to find the narrow path to life. That's where you need to place your energy.

(That's not to say that we look the other way when bad things are happening to other people, or forsake the laws of the land when they are being broken, of course; it's our attitude of judgmentalism that we are considering here, which lets us off the hook even as it seeks to crucify others.)

* * *

Stop to think
We can positively use the moments in which we sense our judgmentalism (and our hackles) rising – when we read a news story about a terrible act, for example – to become aware of our own reaction to others. Think of a time recently when you heard about a 'bad news' story. You may have read one in which the press described someone as a 'monster', for example. How did you end up thinking about that person? Why did you react in the way you did? What emotions did the story stir in you? Could you learn something about yourself through your reaction?

Now imagine you are standing in the crowd that had taken the woman caught in adultery to Jesus. Think about the woman who had done wrong in the eyes of the law. Ask yourself how she might be feeling. How would you have reacted when Jesus said, 'Let the person who is without sin throw the first stone'? If you had been in that crowd, how would you tell the story to a friend who had not been there?

* * *

Unburden yourself

As we begin to experience our own sense of transformation – albeit that we may have simply 'changed one thing' by now – it is vital to remain humble and non-judgmental. Our temptation is naturally to think more highly of ourselves, as we enjoy our personal sense of progress, and to seek to impose that particular change on others. How many ex-smokers go around berating others for lighting up? How many new gym members start telling others that they should get fit? Quite a few, surely.

Our challenge is to maintain the small degrees of change we may have experienced, and to settle gently and assuredly into more of a whole, new way of being, allowing the transformation that others may see in us to do the talking, instead of talking about it.

The good news is that our burden, then, should lift: no longer are we concerned about the speck in our neighbour's eye. We are released from carrying the weight of wanting to change others (though not from carrying the burden of their well-being, which is different). We can travel more lightly, in the knowledge that we only have to worry about one person: ourselves.

That is not to say we lack sympathy or compassion for those we can see are crying out for help in their lives. As we progress, we will have much wisdom to share, as and when we are invited to share it. But for now, simply our presence with those who need us will begin to have a positive, inspiring effect.

The peace we derive (for instance) from becoming a little more still, reflective and focused on our contemplative journey will transmit naturally; it will even help to change the atmosphere in a room. How many people around you seem relentlessly driven, unsettled, stressed? Once upon a time, you may have gone with the flow in such circumstances and allowed yourself to be carried along on the tide of stress yourself – adding to the collective sense of madness. But now, you might notice yourself standing a little more firmly, breathing a little more deeply, and allowing a deeper sense of your presence and rootedness to pervade.

It will have an effect, you can be sure. And it's not just that people will notice a change in *you* – they will also notice how your presence has an effect on *them*. For we cannot help but affect the world around us; the question, always, is how we wish to affect it.

* * *

Start to act

Try a very simple exercise. Next time you walk into a room, make sure you smile. And watch for the reaction from those who are there. Note the effect it has on them. Our presence is contagious, even if we think we are insignificant, unimportant. You are not: your presence is sacred.

If, instead, you walked into the room frowning, what do you

think would happen?

If we can change the atmosphere in a room just by smiling or frowning, how much more can we begin to positively affect those we work or live with in deeper ways, through who we are becoming?

* * *

Salt and light

In his famous 'Sermon on the Mount', Jesus turned received wisdom on its head by suggesting that it was the poor, the meek, the peacemakers and 'those who mourn' who are more likely to see and experience God. 'You are the salt of the earth... You are the light of the world,' he encouraged them.[2]

Salt doesn't go around telling people what to do. Light does not walk around with a stick with which to beat others. Salt preserves and adds flavour; light illuminates. It simply 'is'.

Your presence with others – either directly, as you work or play; or indirectly, as you live your life within your local community – can have a profoundly significant effect; perhaps far more significant than you think.

The psychologist and author Oliver James agrees that small, humble, positive pockets of humanity within communities are akin to the salt and light that Jesus mentioned. 'The people who are spiritual and ethical – they quietly infect everybody else,' he told me once in an interview. 'That's what really interests me; the idea that a small number of people in a community can keep everyone else sane.'

It personally gave me heart. Perhaps people who are 'good' have a disproportionately positive effect on the culture around them, even if (and perhaps especially if) they don't realize it. 'I think so, yes,' he replied.

James went on to suggest that for him, such people were those 'who seem to see through the nonsense of modern life, and who have a good sense of self without being self-focused or narcissistic. They lead by example – being playful, not game-playing; authentic, not sincere; vivacious rather than hyperactive.' It's a helpful description.

Heroes in waiting

If all that sounds a little too passive for your liking, you can look at it another way. The emeritus professor of psychology at Stanford University, Philip Zimbardo, wrote once in an intriguing article in the *Guardian* newspaper that while most people 'conform, yield and succumb' to the negative power of many social situations, 'there are always some who refuse and resist.'

He suggests that it's their *orientation* that counts: such people aim to walk a different path and respond appropriately when they are called to. While some situations spark what he calls a 'hostile imagination' in many, Zimbardo maintains, they provoke the 'heroic imagination' of the few. 'We must teach people to think of themselves as "heroes in waiting",' he wrote, 'ready to take heroic action in a particular situation that may occur only once in their lifetime.'

This helps us to understand the positively outward-looking way that we can express the small degrees of change that happen to us. As we become more spiritually attuned to who we are and how we can act differently, we are better prepared to respond positively in times of crisis or need or difficulty. We are ordinary heroes in waiting, then – not because we have super powers or because we are seeking to change the world according to the way we now see it, but because something deeper within is priming us to be ready, when called to, to make the right choice, or to lend a hand, or to stand up for what is good, or to act self-sacrificially. It is a dynamic, self-giving process, without being prescriptive.

Assured life

We human beings tend to make relentless comparisons with each other, either positively (when we judge people according to our 'higher' or 'superior' standards, as we have already observed) or negatively (when we judge ourselves in the light of others, and find ourselves wanting). In both cases, we set ourselves free when we stop doing so. We are freed from being judgmental of others; but we are also freed from judging ourselves negatively according to the way of the broken world. It works both ways.

As we begin to live more self-assuredly, no longer weighed down by constantly looking at how others act and what they will think of us, we are liberated to become much more fully the people we were created to be in the first place. And that is when our presence becomes most positively felt.

This does not happen overnight, though. Do not be fooled. It is a daily battle – a spiritual battle, if you like – to *be* the change, as Gandhi said, not to preach the change or to force the change or to judge others for not changing as fast as you.

Spreading the love

How do we think most positively about passing on any wisdom as we increasingly tap into the spiritual source of our being? It's worth reflecting on how anything is 'passed on' before we move into a deeper flow through our iconic journey.

We have already reflected on the fact that we affect the world around us, whether we like it or not, either positively or negatively. We are relational beings, and everything we do and everything we are flows through our relationships. A frown is contagious; a smile is infectious. A frenzied presence increases stress; a still, assured presence brings peace.

One generous way of thinking about 'passing on' the benefits of our transformation is through sharing. We can share the benefits of our changing self with those around us – through generosity, kindness, meekness, humility, vision, stillness, presence, service. We can look to share ourselves with others both by demonstrating who we are becoming and by giving ourselves away – sharing with those who need us most, instead of trying to take our share from them.

Such an orientation leads us relentlessly towards the goal of our journey, which is love. The impulse of most forms of spiritual wisdom is this: love God, and love your neighbour – even your enemy. As we begin to awaken to a new paradigm, we see that we flourish not from living in fear, insecurity or constant comparison, but from the assurance of self-giving love for God and others. And so, if we wish to spread anything, let us spread a positive contagion of hope, in love.

The story we begin to live through our lives, then, is of a love that cannot help but give itself away. As we awaken to greater possibilities within our own lives, as we see the world through fresh eyes and live the change creatively, then we cannot help but bear and share the fruit of such love with others.

Holding lightly to everything that matters

In the film *American Beauty*, the hero, Lester, a 43-year-old man, undergoes a transformation: from a joyless husband and a dulled, work-enslaved man, to someone who has remembered who he really is, and who he wanted to be. At the end of the movie, he is killed. And tragic though this is, the final scene closes with his disembodied voice reflecting on what he has really learned in the last year of his life: the ungraspable nature of beauty.

'It's hard to stay mad when there's so much beauty in the world,' he says. 'Sometimes I feel like I'm seeing it all at once, and it's too much. My heart fills up like a balloon that's about to burst... and then I remember to relax, and stop trying to hold on to it, and then it flows through me like rain and I can't feel anything but gratitude for every single moment of my stupid little life...'

It's a deeply moving finish. And it reminds us that when you try to hold on to the very best things for yourself, you can't. You have to let them pass through you somehow – flow through you, and through those around you. None of us can bottle the beauty of a sunset; it is beyond our grasp, too beautiful almost to describe. None of us can distil the essence of a moment of intimacy with someone we love, or the birth of a child, or the smell of freshly cut grass, or the sight of the ocean. Such experiences can only flow through us like rain.

That is the posture we must adopt as we seek to touch the deeper parts of our life, to build a bridge between our doing and our being, to unlock our spiritual intelligence and begin to touch others in the process. We seek to flourish more as fully human creatures, created neither to judge nor to hoard the best things in life, but to become truly a part of an unfolding vision – of the beauty of everyday, ordinary life. Such an outlook will be a gift to all those you come into contact with.

* * *

Stop to think

One Jewish psalm talks about the person who 'meditates' on God's way – who spends serious time contemplating who they are, in relationship to God and, we might add, to God's creation, to beauty, to love. It takes serious application to do this – to work time into your daily schedule to refresh your 'doing' by reflecting on your 'being'. But this is the result:

> *You're a tree replanted in Eden,*
> *bearing fresh fruit every month,*
>
> *Never dropping a leaf,*
> *always in blossom.*[3]

Spend a few minutes reflecting on what it might mean for you and the people around you if you were to become rooted in this way. Ask yourself what it means to be 'always in blossom' and bearing 'fresh fruit': who would benefit from the fresh fruit in your life? What would that fruit taste like? What does it mean to be like a tree that is 'replanted in Eden'?

Level 2

The false self

Chapter 5

Awakening

*Nobody saw the world as I did, nor did they feel the things I
felt… That has to count for something.*
Douglas Coupland[1]

We ended the last chapter by reflecting on the ungraspable nature
of beauty, and the idea that if we are to pass on the benefits of
any personal transformation through nurturing our spiritual
intelligence, then they must flow like rain through us – not be
hoarded, or used as a measure by which we may favourably
compare ourselves with others.

Now we turn to the second level of the journey, and we find
ourselves back where we started – considering the art of awakening,
but from a deeper perspective. And what better place to begin than
by continuing to think about beauty?

For it is our awakening to the beauty around us that puts us in
touch with those deeper places within. It is impossible to explain
why we feel moved to the core on the occasions when we are
confronted by a truly sublime sight, or taste, or smell, or touch, or
sound; but we are. Such moments evoke a yearning within us: they
tug us, draw us, usher us into a different realm, and for a few brief
moments, the world outside and inside of us is transformed into
something truly different.

* * *

Stop to think
Before we continue, think of a time when you felt deeply moved,
emotionally or spiritually. What was it that prompted you to feel
that way? How did you feel? And how did you react? How long

was it before the moment was 'lost'? Why were you not able to continue within the bliss of the moment?

* * *

Beauty is gift

The spiritual writer John Eldredge suggests that 'we need not fear indulging here. The experience of beauty is unique to all the other pleasures in this: there is no possessive quality to it. Just because you love the landscape doesn't mean you have to acquire the real estate... Simply to behold the flower is enough; there is nothing in me that wants to consume it.'

He continues, 'Beauty is the closest thing we have to fullness without possessing on this side of eternity. Perhaps that is why it so healing – beauty is pure gift. It helps in our letting go.'[2]

The experience of beauty awakens us profoundly, despite the fact that, if we try too hard to grasp it (or are confounded by our inability to grasp it), it will slip through our fingers.

Beauty reminds us that the best things in life cannot be owned; they can only be experienced, appreciated and shared. 'Possession', we may therefore deduce, is not the goal of life; the spiritually intelligent response to beauty is to reflect, instead, on why we do not need to possess the greatest things in order to be a part of them. Our ultimate source of identity does not spring from our dominant capitalist world view, which tells us that we need to purchase and consume in order to become who we truly are. Somewhere deep down, something whispers the real alternative: that it is in our nakedness, our stripped-bare self, that we are most fully open to the possibilities of becoming the person we were born to be.

As Eldredge says, 'beauty is gift'. We begin to become more fully human when we cease trying so hard to buy our way to, or even achieve, happiness, and instead embrace the humility and nakedness that we need in order to receive the best the universe has to offer *as a free gift*.

In Matthew's Gospel, Jesus invites his followers to 'consider the lilies of the field, how they grow'. This was no off-the-cuff remark to illustrate a point, but a command to take seriously: 'Consider the beauty of a flower.' And let it speak to you. Accept it as gift, as an opportunity for awakening. 'They neither toil nor spin,' he continued. 'And yet I say to you that even Solomon in all his glory was not arrayed like one of these.'[3]

It is astounding how we manage to close our eyes to the continued blessing of nature-as-gift – a gift which is all around us. It's not just that a simple flower is simply beautiful, or that a flowing river is tranquil, or that a raging sea is awesome; the gift of such a sight or experience speaks of our reconnection with creation and the generosity of its Creator.

It invites us at every turn to stop, slow down, focus, reflect, receive and be transformed by a beauty beyond our faltering grasp. And 'it helps in our letting go.' None of us – not even the richest sheikh or supermodel – can match the beauty of the flowers through what we wear; so why should we strive in our own strength to become outwardly beautiful, when all the time we effuse a very different gift of beauty, the beauty of how we were made?

We will think specifically about how we can begin to 'let go' in Chapter 7. For letting go is the key to letting good things flow, like rain, throughout our lives. For now, it is important simply to note that if we are to extend the lessons of nature-as-gift beyond a few fleeting moments of transcendence, we should allow its ungraspable essence to counsel us in the art of holding more lightly to the things of this life. For we will have to surrender everything, ultimately, in the greatest act of letting go: our death.

* * *

Start to act
Spend at least 15 minutes outside reflecting on the beauty of a flower or something beautifully simple and simply beautiful. Ask what it says to you about life. What does it teach you? How might you grasp what you learn within the busyness of your everyday life, without holding it too tightly?

* * *

A space to explore

> *God is nowhere.*
> *God is now here.*

Just the tiniest of spaces can make the world of difference to our perception of the universe. And sometimes, all we need to do is afford ourselves a little space to explore that intriguing tension between what is 'nowhere' and 'now here'.

As we begin to awaken to beauty around us, we may sense a connection to something, or Someone, higher than ourselves. Beauty speaks to us of goodness and of God. At the very least, it reminds us that there is surely more to life than meets the eye; that there is a bewildering mystery to the universe, which has a capacity to stop us in our tracks and challenge us to take stock, to rethink who we are in relation to what we see around us.

Such moments, however, bring into sharper contrast the everyday experience we have of life, which so often seems far from divine. We may go to the mountain top for a sublime experience, but what happens when we have to descend, once more, into the valley below?

This is the crux of any truly spiritually intelligent awakening. For in a way, it is easy to rise to the challenge of beauty, and allow yourself to be captivated by those fleeting, sublime moments. It is harder to search for, and awaken to, the sacred within the mundane; to identify beauty in the ugly places of the world, or in the deadly boring routines, or in the times when we feel at our lowest.

For much of our lives, it really can seem to appear that God is 'nowhere'. The biblical book of Ecclesiastes embraces such a feeling and explores it. 'Everything is meaningless,' says the writer. 'Completely meaningless.'[4] The text expresses what most of us think or feel at some point in our life. Whether it's the agony of a close friend dying or simply the monotony of a stultifying job or routine, it can often feel as if there is little more to life than boredom, pain or sorrow.

Our lowest moments can also, conversely, prompt us to awaken to reality: to the fact that life on this earth does not go on forever, that none of us are invincible, that we must confront the question of who we are and where we're going if we're to become more fully human. And we can use such times to explore the need to look outwards – to something, or Someone, beyond us – to help bring meaning to our present and hope for our future.

But perhaps for now, the secret is simply to inhabit the tiny space created between 'God is nowhere' and 'God is now here'. It is a creative tension that does not even necessarily need to be resolved; merely acknowledged and inhabited. We are often so afraid of space, even a little space. Sometimes, we must confront and embrace it.

* * *

Stop to think
Do you gravitate most naturally towards the phrase 'God is nowhere' or 'God is now here'? Why? Think of the times when you have experienced the opposite. What does the little 'space' mean to you? How can you use it to awaken to the reality of God being both 'nowhere' and 'now here'?

* * *

Life as a whole

> *Life is holy, and every moment precious.*
> **Jack Kerouac**[5]

As we continue on the journey towards becoming more fully human, the truth we can awaken to most powerfully is that all of life is spiritual. God does not just live in churches or temples. We do not simply experience transcendence when we sit at the top of the mountain. We should try not to see our lives as somehow compartmentalized – boxed up, if you like. Instead, life is one continuous path, through work, family, friends, church, hobbies, politics, community, everything. You can, after all, only place one foot in front of the other.

Life doesn't matter on the whole – it matters *as* a whole. In today's culture, it's so easy to 'be' different people within the many different social environments in which we find ourselves. Have you found yourself wishing you weren't so much of a social chameleon, changing who you are to fit with the different people you find yourself with? Have you experienced that awful moment when two worlds collide, when people you act in a certain way with suddenly meet other people you know, with whom you are really quite different? Why do you feel awkward when they meet? It's probably because you are afraid of being found out; that at least one set of friends will not quite recognize who you are within that different setting.

Of course, it's perfectly natural to behave a little differently with your workmates than with your parents; but if there is no central point to you – no essence, no soul, if you like – then you are very unlikely to provide those around you with the gift of true presence. Integrity is about wholeness – all of your parts being integrated within your one self. And it's usually those with integrity who manage to make their presence felt for good within the world. It's an attractive thing to know, and to be known, for who you really are.

* * *

Stop to think
If you were to put people from all your different social circles in a room together, what stories would they tell about who you are, how you act, what kind of things you say, what your ambitions are, and so on? Which stories would you find most awkward? Which of your friends or colleagues would you be most afraid of introducing to each other? What first steps could you make to begin to act with greater integrity towards all of the people you know?

* * *

There's more to you than meets the eye

When we talk about integrity and wholeness, we introduce the idea that we have the potential to be 'whole'. Now, this can mean whole like a jigsaw – in that all our parts are together and nothing is missing. This, in itself, is a good thing to awaken to. We are mind, body, soul and more… and there is no one part of us that is more 'me' or 'you' than anything else. We are individual ecosystems, incredible communities of cells, tissue, bone, muscle, blood, organs, feelings, thoughts, senses, yearnings, soul, mind, spirit...

You may be a brilliant musician or writer or dancer or secretary. But that's not ultimately who you are, it's what you do. You may be very good looking, or less so – but that's not ultimately who you are, either. Your physical appearance is not everything. You may be blind or deaf, you may be uptight or laid back, you may be known and loved for your cooking, or berated for your lack of it! But that's not the whole you. Beware allowing others to label you, or labelling yourself, according to your outstanding features, talents or tendencies.

So we are whole, like a completed jigsaw. But being 'whole' also involves so much more. Being whole is about well-being: being at peace with yourself within each situation you find yourself in (and not feeling that awkwardness when worlds collide). Being whole is about healing: letting go of old wounds and moving gracefully and graciously towards becoming the person you were put on earth to be. Being whole is about coming to know and understand that you have been made whole, and that you do not need to strive harder and harder to reach that wholeness, but instead to stop striving and start being. It is about knowing who you are, and acting from the very core of who you are, in love and service.

We will explore more deeply the idea of wholeness in Chapter 9, when we think about awakening to the possibilities of living from your 'whole' self. For now, let's simply remember that on our journey towards becoming more fully human, we journey towards wholeness. But before we awaken to who we are, we must first awaken to who we are not. And that, in itself, is a serious challenge.

<u>Things you are not: No. 1</u>
You are not a consumer of this world (you are in communion with it)

> *You're not your job. You're not how much money you have in the bank. You're not the car you drive. You're not the contents of your wallet. You're not your f**king khakis.*
> **Tyler Durden, Fight Club**

It seems so true, when you see the words of Tyler Durden, the hero of *Fight Club*, written down: you are *not* your job – thank goodness – even though you may spend much of your time introducing yourself by what you do, not who you are, and drawing a strange sense of pride from the kudos (if you do something interesting; you may, conversely, feel embarrassed if you don't 'do' anything exciting or intriguing for a 'living').

Ask yourself what you would do if you were made redundant tomorrow: how would you react? How overstretched would you find yourself? How humiliated would you feel? How much of a challenge would it be to your deep-down sense of who you really are?

It all depends on how 'attached' you have become to the way your job contributes to your sense of identity – and how highly you value the identity it actually bestows. If you have identified yourself too closely with your place or role in life, then if you lose it, you will be left with nothing but who you really are… And we all need to be prepared for the eventuality of being stripped naked by the forces and fortunes of life. For we are being stripped, whether we like it or not. As Tyler famously says elsewhere in the film, 'This is your life, and it's ending one minute at a time.'

You may read his words and assent to them in theory. But can you really say that you're '*not* how much money you've got in the bank'? How differently do you feel about yourself – or about others – when you (or they) have accumulated significant wealth, and vice versa? Don't we treat rich people differently – just in case we can get something out of them?

And don't we feel more self-satisfied if we've just received a pay rise, or a bonus? It's time for us to awaken, not to the fact that money is evil, but to the fact that 'the love of money is a root of all kinds of evil', as the apostle Paul is reputed to have said.[6] It's our 'attachment' to it – and to the sense of identity and value we allow it to bestow on us – that is dangerous. For when we look at other people and see their money, or their power, or their social position – instead of who they are – then we judge them accordingly, and usually, we make rapid decisions about what we can get out of them (even if simply by association).

If we judge ourselves, meanwhile, by our earning power, or by how well known we are, and if we feel as if we need to prove ourselves constantly by earning more, or becoming more famous, or climbing higher up the ladder, then we mistake ourselves for someone we are not.

You're not the car you drive, nor the car you dream of driving. You're not an Aston Martin or a Mercedes or Ferrari... Of course, your car says *something* about you – the question is, what do you let it say? 'I need a car to prove I'm really someone'?

And you're not your khakis – the clothes you wear, the look you fashion. You may think you can buy yourself an off-the-peg identity, and in a sense we are all engaged in the art of image management; but the clothes we buy will never truly cover our insecurities or inadequacies or fears or phobias like a fig leaf, nor will they ever turn us into the person we hope to become. They may impress other people who derive their own sense of value from outward appearances – but God looks on the inside of a person, not at the label.

* * *

Stop to think

Remember, we're talking about awakening to the person we're not. What are the props you use to create an identity for yourself, in particular? Which thing do you hide behind the most – your job, your wealth, your car, your clothes, something you've bought? Who has most to gain all the while you continue to believe the myth that you need to earn more, or buy yourself an identity, or seek your self-worth from your social position? Whose interests does that person, or that company, or that magazine, or that TV programme, have at heart?

What might happen if you changed the way you saw yourself?

If this really is 'your life' and 'it's ending minute by minute', how can you grow most effectively – by accumulating things, or by letting them go? At what point do you stop pretending and start living as the person you really are, beneath all the layers you've built up to defend yourself?

* * *

The Archbishop of Canterbury, Dr Rowan Williams, wrote a profound sentence about this that we shall explore further in the next chapter. He wrote, 'We are not consumers of this world; we are in communion with it.'

While the retailers and multinationals and moneylenders (and all the other people with most to gain from consumer culture) see you as a consumer, end of story, your innate spiritual intelligence whispers something else to you, deep down within. 'I am not a target market,' it says. No, you are not. You are not. You are not.

We must avoid defining ourselves exclusively by that which we are not. But this is part of the process of being stripped bare, as each minute passes.

<u>Things you are not: No. 2</u>
You are not in competition (you are cooperative)

> *You lack the guts needed to face it,*
> *Say goodbye to the way you've been living.*
> *You never realized you were on the wrong side*
> *And nobody's going to win.*
> **Jarvis Cocker, 'From A to I'**

From the day we are born, we are taught to compete. It's often drilled into us subconsciously by proud parents boasting about how soon their baby has walked, or talked; or how fast they learned to read and write; or how they've made the first team; or how they are taller or smarter or more polite or better behaved than the girl or boy down the road, or in their class, or on their team, or on the opposition.

We grow up learning to play the same old game by the same old rules – there are winners and losers, and you'd better end up a winner, because the winner gets the spoils. Remember the shame you felt if you were the last to be picked for a team sport? Loser.

And so, we begin (and end) by seeing the world through the lens of victory and defeat, and we learn to feel the fear of failing an exam and of being 'found out' as a loser, or being left off the team, or simply being unpopular. So we do whatever we can to make sure our cover isn't blown – whether that's by cheating or paying others to do our work for us, or covering up the truth or distracting people's attention from the fraud we really believe we are… (Did you know that one of the most common fears among chief executives is that of 'being found out'?)

And our scriptures and sacred texts tell us, all the while, that the first will be last and the last will be first; that you need to *lose* your life in order to win. It's upside-down, inside-out wisdom; in fact, spiritual intelligence demands that you question the order of *everything*, if you are willing to listen carefully enough to the still, small voice in your heart.

* * *

Stop to think

Who are the real winners in life? Don't think of the right answer, necessarily, but of a person you know who exemplifies what it truly means to be a 'winner'.

How do they help to redefine the idea of being a 'winner'?

When we become focused on winning, what happens to our attitude to 'the opposition' or 'the competition'? Who are they? Who is your 'competition', and what do you think of them?

What enemies have you created, in your own mind, through playing the same old game by the same old rules? What enemies has your company created, or your culture, or your country? How does this affect you, and your enemy?

Why did Jesus say, 'Love your enemies'? Who says who are the winners and losers, the friends and enemies?

What does it feel like to be an enemy? What does it feel like to be a loser?

* * *

Start to act

We are born to compete, and when others die, we usually judge them in terms of how they've fared in the game of life. We judge their 'success' by their achievements, their awards, their accolades, their wealth, the size of their house, the way other people talk about them, and so on.

Do you wish to be remembered as someone who played the same old game by the same old rules, even if that makes you a 'winner' in the eyes of the world? If not, how would you like to rewrite the rules? How would you like to change the game?

Take some time to write your own obituary. This could be a very profound time of awakening for you, so take it slow, and do it well. You might even try writing from a few different angles:

Try writing about the person you were not.

Try not to write it from the angle of winning and losing, but from a different perspective. (What should the balance of judgment be between things you have achieved and the person you became?)

Try writing the one you'd most like people to read.

Try writing the one you think will be written about you by others.

If you only had space for an epitaph, not an obituary, what would it be?

* * *

Things you are not: No. 3
You are not a comparison (you are incomparable)

I want to return to Oliver James for this section. He told me that 'human beings can be tempted by the ultimate in satanic ways of social esteem, of wanting to feel that they are successful *in relation to their fellow men*, and that those comparisons can be manipulated in such a way as to become central to one's whole purpose'.

That's heavy stuff, but fascinating nevertheless: 'social esteem' can be seen as a bad idea that we can fall for (and *not* something we should necessarily accept as normal). Moreover, by comparing ourselves to others, we leave ourselves vulnerable to believing that the outcome of such comparison should drive our ultimate quest for success in life.

This is what James calls 'maladapted social comparison' – which can be dangerous and debilitating. The crucial thing is to ask yourself whether your motives for craving money or beauty or high social status or fame (which are, in themselves, 'neutral') are intrinsic or extrinsic. Intrinsic motives are more spiritual and inward; extrinsic ones are about the surface appearance of things.

James is a child psychologist. 'In the first six years,' he suggests, 'it's very possible to care for your children in such a way that they are extremely vulnerable to feeling insecure [when faced with] all the social prizes that are around in our society.' We set our children up to compare themselves with everyone around them.

And what we learn in childhood, we take into adulthood. We compare ourselves relentlessly with those around us – our looks, our things, our intellect, our likeability – and we constantly find ourselves wanting. We find ourselves wanting more and more, to keep up with the Joneses, to prove that we have what it takes, to demonstrate to a watching world that we are outwardly successful *in comparison with everyone else.*

James, who spent time researching the effects of maladapted social comparison for his books *Affluenza* and *Selfish Capitalism*, did see an antidote, however.

An intrinsic, spiritual understanding of who you are and from where you seek your identity can have great benefits. 'I have to say,' he confessed, 'that I was really surprised, again and again, to find that spirituality (while not the only thing) was a significant component in helping people.'

Perhaps that's because our spiritual intelligence tells us that if we compare ourselves favourably with others, we must savour their lower status as well as exalting our own. In a culture of comparison, you need those who compare less favourably in order to see yourself (and be seen by others) in a favourable light. Extrinsic social comparison feeds our paranoia and insecurity. It looks at the surface of things and fails to take us deeper, into the realm of celebrating our incomparable uniqueness, as individual, interconnected people made in the image of God.

It's different, of course, to look at the intrinsic worth of others, and to ask searching questions of yourself in the light of the way other inspiring people live. We must awaken to our motives for comparing ourselves to others. One is about looking good, seeming successful, attaching ourselves to outward trappings; the other is about inner growth, being well, and detaching ourselves from the things that hinder.

* * *

Things you are not: No. 4
You are not your ego

For many years, a phrase in the great book *Generation X* by Douglas Coupland intrigued and troubled me. He simply wrote in capital letters in the margin of one his chapters, 'YOU ARE NOT YOUR EGO.'

As we now try to see our world through different eyes – understanding who we are not – this is the truly great thing we need to awaken to. We are not our ego.

We began this particular discussion by thinking about what it means to be whole. We considered how being whole can involve all the parts being fitted together like a jigsaw, and that being whole should lead on to health, well-being, healing, integrity, soulfulness – 'wholeness'.

One of our greatest dangers is to mistake the incessant chattering of our minds for the person we really are. We begin the next chapter by asking what it means to see your world not from the single perspective of your ego, but from other, undiscovered places inside and outside you.

* * *

Stop to think

For now, simply stop, and notice what's on your mind, aside from the content of this book. What else is racing through it right now? Write down everything that 'comes to mind'.

Chapter 6

Seeing afresh

Spirituality is a life-filled path, a spirit-filled way of living...
A path is the way itself and every moment on it is a holy moment;
a sacred seeing goes on there.
Matthew Fox[1]

The art of awakening, and then of seeing the world through fresh eyes, is about becoming aware, one step at a time. The process cannot be rushed, by definition. It does not happen instantaneously. It is not something you can buy off the shelf.

Instead, it's about stopping to notice things – and capitalizing on what you have noticed. As you become more deeply aware, your awareness will begin to change you and those around you for good. It's that simple.

We receive gifts of awakening every day of our lives, but most of them remain unopened. How many times have you experienced something special – a moment of ecstasy, a deeply moving book or film, a challenging conversation, a weird coincidence, a child's smile – but let it pass without serious reflection? That's frequently because we are either too busy or, as we will now consider, because our minds are too active to settle us meaningfully into the rhythm of what is unfolding at a deeper level.

So, as you awaken, try to notice what is happening to you. Write it down. Reflect on it. Try not to let the moment pass. You will begin to spot those gifts of awakening in places you'd previously walked through with your eyes closed. You will start to walk through those same places with your eyes wider open.

And so, we move into seeing with fresh eyes, on level 2 of the journey. How will you begin to see the world around you afresh, having reflected on who you are *not*?

We must begin where we left off: with the ego.

You are not your ego, continued

This is simple enough – there is no need to confuse our reflection here on the ego with complex and difficult theories. That would be to fall foul of trying to make things more impressive than they need to be, which is what the ego begs us to do, daily. Here is the essence of something I wish I'd been told when I was growing up.

We live in a fallen state of grace. The Bible teaches that humanity's relationship with God has been fractured, dislocated – as has our relationship with others, the planet and ourselves. From the cradle to the grave, we experience varying levels of pain, frustration, fragmentation, fear, meaninglessness, disease and death. Sometimes, we can be sheltered from the more physical manifestations of our fallen state, especially in the West. Nevertheless, our lives can often seem like a struggle – a struggle, in particular, to derive meaning and identity from what can feel like a cruel, pointless or random set of circumstances unfolding around us, conspiring against us.

We may simply struggle to get out of bed in the morning with a spring in our step; to head purposefully to work; to love what we do, and do it with all our heart; to make the most of our time, whatever we're doing; to treat people as we'd like to be treated ourselves; to be gracious and forgiving against the odds; to exude creativity and innovation; to live at peace with ourselves; to be fully present with our friends and family... Life can be a struggle when it's not you who's in control.

It's all in the mind

So who *is* in control? You may be surprised.

Our mind is one of our best means of defence within this 'fallen' world. Subconsciously, it seeks to create for us a sense of identity, which protects us like armour and uses props to form a meaningful story out of what is going on around us. The mind is a valuable and essential tool, of course, and when used appropriately, it is vital to our well-being. But when it is driven – or over-driven, to be more precise – by our sense of pain and fear, we can find it almost impossible to switch off.

And that's when we begin to mistake the incessant commentary in our head – our ego – for who we really are. It comments, it judges, it critiques, it plans, it refuses to forget. It rarely lets us settle into any present moment; instead it keeps dragging us back to the past, or plotting our course to the future – whether that's what we're going to do at the weekend or how we're going to afford a bigger house.

Our ego 'attaches' itself to things around us – possessions are the most obvious choice, but look out for the way it also clings to pride, prestige, power… all sorts of things that can create an identity for you, making a *someone* out of your particular no one. This is you, it tells you. You are what you own, what you have achieved; you are your past hurts (just wait until you get revenge), as well as the good things that people have said of you, that make you feel like you're worth it.

The ego creates weapons of attack and defence. Locked in survival mode, it seeks to defend you and attack the reputation or ability or record of those around you. 'You're better than that person,' it will tell you. 'Look at them… Look what they're doing! Honestly…'

Eckhart Tolle suggests that 'you can assume that virtually everyone you meet or know lives in a state of fear. Only the intensity of it varies. It fluctuates between anxiety and dread at one end of the scale and a vague unease and distant sense of threat at the other. Most people only become conscious of it when it takes on one of its most acute forms.'[2]

Remember, this is about seeing with fresh eyes: seeing those around us afresh, as people who – like us – are fearful and driven by their egocentric defence mechanism. It is about seeing who we really are, and understanding in a deeper, more enlightened way that we are not the incessant, chattering voice in our head, but something more expansive.

* * *

Listening for the music within

I remember the days when I used to play in a rock band. We had to arrive at the little venues in London around 5 p.m., and there would usually be three or four other bands on the bill. All the bands would arrive at roughly the same time, and you'd have to wait around together as the equipment was set up and each band went through its soundcheck.

It was a terrifying ritual, in its own way. You were about to stand on stage and play your own songs to an unknown audience and to rival bands. And this is precisely the kind of situation when the ego does its business most effectively. As I listened to the others going through their soundchecks, I would hear a voice inside my head (which I would usually articulate at great speed to my band mates) saying, 'They're not as good as us. They don't have the songs. They're not very tight. Look at the way they dress. We're better than them.'

And I would pose, adopting a persona to cope with the pressure, trying to seem cooler than I was. The band itself provided me with a sense of identity that I treasured and could boast about and didn't ever want to lose. It allowed me to believe I was special, set apart, in the spotlight, talented, *someone*. (And who knows? Perhaps even by using this example within this book, I'm subconsciously still trying to prove my worth to you in some way, hinting that I must be OK and cool and culturally engaged because I used to be in a band that played some very good small venues in London...)

At the time, if I'd been more self-assured and generous in spirit, I would have been able to switch that voice off, relax, breathe deeply, and play to my best. As it was, it was hard. And it was also such a shame. It meant I couldn't ever really enjoy those nights as I should have done, in the spirit of cooperation and communion that music should really be all about.

The example continues, too: our goal was to be signed to a record label; to get a deal, and become 'recognized'. Rehearsals were a means to an end – of getting 'tighter' so that gigs were polished and professional. And gigs were the means to the end of getting signed. We would look constantly to see if the 'industry' contacts had shown up; we got upset by little mistakes; we were gutted if not enough people came to see us; we would get edgy with each other, knowing we had to play well to give ourselves a chance of succeeding – and we tensed up in the process and probably made more mistakes than we'd have otherwise made...

Once we reached the age when we were too old to be signed as a band, we gave up trying to impress, left the ego to one side, and – lo and behold – started to really enjoy ourselves. We saw rehearsals as a chance to experiment, socialize, regenerate; gigs became a chance to listen to other music, see old friends, play from the heart and continue a tradition of 'folk' music that was never meant to be about fame or limousines or adulation or recordings. It was a revelation: we let go, surrendered our vain ambition, and in the process, discovered something infinitely more precious than a record contract – something that had been there all the time, if only we'd allowed ourselves to recognize and experience it.

* * *

Stop to think
When does your ego respond most obviously to a state of heightened fear? Is there one situation in particular when you repeatedly find yourself responding directly from the defensive ego? What kinds of thing do you end up saying? Or thinking?

* * *

Most of us have developed our own weapons of defence and attack. I remember a particularly insecure teacher of mine, who used a fearsome combination of sarcastic humour and incomprehensible Latin phrases to assert his supremacy in the classroom. He was driven by fear, and determined to make us fear him in the process (see how it gets passed on?). You never knew when you'd be picked upon, or made to feel stupid, or simply mystified by words you'd never heard before.

Our weapons become most obvious when we are under pressure. But we use them all the time, in subtle ways. You might have been using them without ever recognizing what you have been doing. (That's why awakening, becoming more aware, is in itself a sacred act, of growth and love and surrender.)

Do you put people down through humour? Do you use names to belittle people? Do you identify yourself with so many acts of care for others that no one can care for you? Do you run your company through fear and try to command obedience with the threat of punishment or demotion or the sack? Are you so determined to prove yourself to your parents or friends or detractors that you never stop for a moment to reflect on what *you*'d like to achieve in life?

The voice in your head never seems to stop for a moment, from first thing in the morning to last thing at night. And if we wake in the night, it's even harder to turn it off; it seems more acute, filling us with worries about tomorrow, or dwelling on the things people have said to hurt us today, replaying highlights from the day that generate a sense of wounded identity or pride... Why do things always seem worse at night? Perhaps it's because we get the unadulterated voice of the ego coming through to us, in all its pain and fear.

We feel it in our bodies – the stress and strain, the negative emotions, even simply the sense of being driven, driven, driven, to succeed. The body manifests our emotions, which are generated in major part by the ego responding to the events unfolding around it.

* * *

Start to feel
Stop, for a moment, and feel how you *feel*. Is your jaw relaxed or tense? What about your shoulders? How are you 'holding' your body? Where are the places of tension? What's your default setting? Do you grind your teeth at night? Try to relax your body, and feel the difference. Simply notice it for a while.

* * *

Stop to think
It is vital to begin to recognize this voice. It's not that hard, to be honest, but it's hard to keep remembering that the ego is so active. Begin to notice what it says, and how often. We'll do a little bit of that in the next chapter. But you might like to think about what the words and phrases and reactions in your head reveal about your ego: fear of failure, of not being recognized, of losing, of being left behind, of being insignificant, of not pleasing your father or mother, of missing the mark...

* * *

We can call this sense of self – derived exclusively from the mind, and manifested as emotions through our bodies – the 'false self'. It is not the whole picture of who we are, merely the part that receives almost all of our attention. It is not our whole, nor does our attention to its incessant chattering lead us into wholeness.

'You are cut off from Being as long as your mind takes up all your attention,' writes Tolle. 'When this happens – and it happens continuously for most people – you are not in your body. The mind absorbs all your consciousness and transforms it into mind stuff. You cannot stop thinking.

'Compulsive thinking has become a collective disease,' he continues. 'Your whole sense of who you are is then derived from mind activity. Your identity, as it is no longer rooted in Being, becomes a vulnerable and ever-needy mental construct, which creates fear as the predominant underlying emotion. The one thing that truly matters is then missing from your life: awareness of your deeper self – your invisible and indestructible reality.'[3]

You are in communion and cooperation; and you are incomparable

As we begin to see ourselves in a new light, we may glimpse fresh ways of being and becoming the person we were created to be. In a consumer culture, the ego will seek to create an identity from the things we buy or own. But if you see yourself primarily in this light, as a consumer, eventually you will be consumed – by greed, dissatisfaction, the constant comparison with those around you; if you see yourself in communion instead – with God, yourself, the planet and others – then you will draw from a positively different source of values.

You need not see yourself in perpetual competition but in cooperation: cooperation is the outworking of communion; if communion is being, cooperation is doing together.

You need not compare yourself extrinsically with others; you are you, and not enough people know that! You may, of course, wish to compare yourself intrinsically, to be inspired by those great women and men who have made a true, positive difference to the world, and whom you admire; but try, always, to understand and celebrate your unique identity. Essentially, critically, you have what it takes. You do not need to look to others for your validation; they will most likely judge you from their own ego, anyway. Remember, you were made to be incomparable, so give up trying to compare yourself now, and start to enjoy being you.

Wholly in communion

Wholeness is about being connected, or reconnected – to others, to God, to the planet, to yourself. And so we remain incomplete if we believe that our journey towards wholeness is to be made in isolation. We remain incomplete if we believe that all of the answers lie entirely within ourselves. And we also remain incomplete if we see the people around us in terms of winners and losers, one of us or 'one of them', and everything around us as if it can be bought or sold for a price.

As we grow increasingly aware of the ego, our perspective must necessarily begin to shift: the world does not revolve around us (though we are a vital part of our world, of course), and we must begin to make the necessary adjustments.

It is possible to see things differently. We cannot go on seeing people as human resources to use (and abuse), as commodities, or as competition. If we are only interested in what others can do for us, or what they can give us, or how they can support us, then we will not grow towards wholeness. Instead, we need the oxygen of communion with others.

We may be individually made up of pieces which fit together, like a jigsaw – mind, body, spirit and the like. But we are also one whole piece of a much bigger puzzle. The apostle Paul refers to 'the body' – which is a better image all together. When we are in communion with others, we are organically connected; if one part hurts, the rest knows it; if one part is missing, the whole is incomplete; and no one part is more or less important, whether it stands out or not.

* * *

Stop to think
How do you see the people who are a part of your life?

Do you tend to give to, or take from, them? Are there some

people you tend to 'take from' more than others? Are there some whom you end up 'giving to' most of the time?

Do you get to know people because they might be 'useful' to you in the long run?

Spend a few minutes on a social audit: write down the names of your family and friends, and ask yourself who benefits most and least from your presence. Are there some people you may need to get back in touch with and try to give more of yourself to? Are there some people you find draining, whom you may need to challenge to speak less of themselves and take more of an active interest in you?

Think of one person you need to give yourself to, and resolve to get in touch.

Think of one person who gives themself unselfishly to you. Be thankful for them.

* * *

'I' before ego

Our identity is shaped in relation to the people we know. But as we seek to transcend our ego, we must not lose sight of who we are in relation to those other people. We do not disappear simply because we are trying to become more whole.

Those people who have reflected deeply upon who they really are have a strength and presence about them that enables them to give of themselves (instead of constantly taking) – *without ever losing their strength or identity*.

Instead of becoming the person everyone else wants them to be, they know who they are becoming, in relation to God, themselves, others and the planet, and they are able to relate to others through self-giving love.

As Mike Riddell suggests, 'Love proceeds from self-knowledge. Only when we truly know ourselves are we free to give ourselves to others. And when that happens, we discover that we are able to give without losing anything... When love proceeds from wholeness, it operates in freedom and generosity. Our partners are regarded not as a means to satisfying our own needs but as the beloved.'[4]

And as the poet Kahlil Gibran writes,

Love one another but make not a bond of love:
Let it rather be a moving sea between the shores of your souls.
Fill each other's cups but drink not from one cup.
Give one another of your bread but eat not from the same loaf.
Sing and dance together and be joyous, but let each
of you be alone,
Even as the strings of a lute are alone though they quiver with
the same music.[5]

I am not apart from you. I am a part of you.

We are one, but not the same.

* * *

The daily battle

You are not your ego… so you can lay it down. That's probably the biggest change in how you see yourself that you will ever undergo. It will take a daily battle, and a lifetime of laying it down, battling the voice of our ego, the voice of our enemy (if we allow it to become our enemy). This is where we engage in spiritual battle. It is a battle with ourselves as well as a battle against forces beyond us.

We learn, day by day, small battle by small battle, to become spiritual warriors with a higher cause to fight for and serve. And lest we feel confused by the aggressive feel of the word 'warrior', the priest and author Matthew Fox helpfully explains. He writes:

To me, the key is understanding the distinction between a warrior and a soldier. A Vietnam veteran who volunteered to go to war at 17 described this eloquently: 'When I was in the army, I was a soldier. I was a puppet doing whatever anybody told me to do, even if it meant going against what my heart told me was right. I didn't know nothing about being a warrior until I hit the streets and marched alongside my brothers for something I really believed in. When I found something I believed in, a higher power found me.' He quit being a soldier and became a warrior when he followed his soul's orders, not his officer's; in his case, this meant protesting war and going to jail for it. The late Buddhist

*meditation master Chögyam Trungpa talks about the 'sad and
tender heart of the warrior'. The warrior is in touch with his
heart – the joy, the sadness, the expansiveness of it…*

He concludes, 'The warrior is so much in touch with his heart that
he can give it to the world.'[6]

This now becomes a purposeful life. You are entering a life of
many small deaths. But then, your life is ending every minute,
anyway. So it's time to use your time wisely, and to fight for
something you believe in.

Now, we'll begin to ask how.

Chapter 7

Living the change

*It's hard to lead a cavalry charge if you think
you look funny on a horse…*
**Adlai Ewing Stevenson,
American politician and statesman**

So now it's time to take some small steps towards 'living it out' at this next level. This is where it begins to get serious, as they say. We have thought about awakening to new level-2 possibilities, and seeing the world differently as a result. But if we don't capitalize on these movements as we travel through the iconic grid, then ideas will remain just words on the page, or locked in our head. Now is our chance for action – remember, change never happens in the past or the future, but always in the present. Today is the day of our salvation.

Think about it like this: any great people you admire have had to learn to walk, literally and metaphorically – one foot in front of the other, one step at a time. They didn't simply arrive at a great life well lived, thanks to a Herculean effort to better themselves. Instead, their lives are comprised of small, sustainable acts of self-giving love that begin to add up to a life's work.

However, the goal is *not* to become 'great'; our journey is less about 'getting there' (in the sense of 'Wow, you've *arrived*') than about the Way you get there. In fact, the Way you travel will determine where you arrive, in the end.

* * *

Stop to think
Think of a journey you've been on, an exciting or epic adventure

you've undertaken – whether that's a literal trip through time and space, or a 'life journey' or 'soul journey' – where you've been through significant or testing times and come out stronger the other side.

Reflect simply on how you set out. What were the first few steps you took? How did you feel as you went? If you looked at those first steps in isolation from the rest of the journey, how would they seem? Would you have experienced the drama along the Way if you hadn't have set out in the first place?

* * *

What's hard about 'living it out' at this level is that we will have to practise something almost entirely unheard of within our culture. It'll take great resolve. You will need courage and dedication. But this is both the hardest *and* the easiest journey to embark upon. The forces of consumerism and competition and comparison will line up squarely against you. (But you have what it takes for the battle.) Your friends may think you are mad. (But do you care?) And the voice in your head won't like it at all.

It's immeasurably hard and effortlessly easy at the same time, because you will have to practise doing… nothing. Absolutely jack.

As you move from contemplation into action, it's not about frantically doing more, but about aligning your doing with your true sense of being. The channel between the two is what we might call 'soul' – and as we pay greater attention to it, that channel will begin to clear and widen; our spiritual intelligence will help us to flow seamlessly between the two, back and forth.

And the way to align your being to your doing is to stop, and step out of the matrix you've created for yourself and around your self – that false reality we touched on in Chapter 5, of all your attachments – and to practise being yourself. It's about time, isn't it?

* * *

Stop to think
When you set out on a journey, you have to leave things behind. Think back to the journey that you just reflected on above. What did you have to leave behind as you set out? What did you

discover you'd lost by the time you arrived at your destination?

How much did you miss those things at first? How much do you miss them now?

* * *

What have you got to lose?

It's an important question. What have you got to lose by letting go of some of the attachments that create your false sense of self? On one level, you have an awful *lot* to lose – that's why few of us really want to go there. Potentially, you may need to let go of many things to which you have become deeply, mistakenly attached. It is time to stop being defined by them.

You must reflect closely on what you *have* to lose if you are to begin to win back your true identity, your true self. That process, of turning away and letting go, can be called 'repentance'. We'll think more about this before moving on. But take it slowly and seriously. For at its most profound level, you have an identity to surrender, the image your ego has created on your behalf.

The good news (and this is all about good news, by the way) is that on another level, you'll find, as you loosen your grip on that image and the voice that creates it, that you have nothing to lose whatsoever, and everything to gain.

* * *

Stop to think

How do you define yourself at the moment? Which 'things' have come to define you over the course of your life? How would other people describe you if they were asked, and how many of your 'attachments' – to possessions, pride, power, prestige and performance – would they identify as key to who they think you are?

Be honest: which attachments do you cling to most strongly as you try to show others who you are? It might be an old hurt, or a material possession, or a job, or other people's praise, as we thought about in Chapter 6.

Spend a few minutes simply noticing these things. You might like to write them on a piece of paper, scrunch it up in your fist, hold on for a few moments, then gradually release your grip and let it fall into a waste paper bin (or the recycling!).

You've seen pictures of astronauts playfully letting things go in space – their toothbrush or a clipboard or food... You might prefer to imagine you are holding on to your attachment in space, in zero gravity. Let it go, gently, and watch it, in your mind's eye, float gently off and spin into space.

* * *

Have you ever wondered what you are trying to escape from?

When we stop our mind from working frenetically, we almost always sense relief. When we have a drink or two, or drift off to sleep, or focus on a task, we 'switch off'. Positively speaking, if we set our mind intensely on one captivating task, such as painting a picture or climbing a rock face, we are drawn into the present moment, and become absorbed, and alive. The trouble is, usually our escapism is not particularly positive, and does not bring about ultimate relief. The voice returns, and so we become addicted to the temporary methods we find – such as having a drink – of shutting it out.

The spiritual life is not just another form of escape, though many people treat it as such. They use it as a drug, like TV. It kills time, distracts them from reality, gives them a future hope of permanent escape. But spiritual intelligence, our soulfulness, should not give us a ticket out of here – in fact, it should give us one straight back in, but in a way that transforms the way we see everything. In the Christian world view, the incarnation of God in the person of Jesus Christ points towards the embrace of, not escape from, life. As the author Eugene Peterson writes, 'God became flesh and blood and moved into the neighbourhood.' By reconnecting our doing with our being, we can remember how to embrace reality. We can learn to face it head on, in quiet, embodied strength.

There is a profound mystery at the heart of life, a creative tension that we are invited to explore in order to discover who we are and how we connect to the world around us: we have to surrender who we think we are in order to discover who we always were. We have to lose our life (as we know it), in order to find it.

And we can only do this if we give ourselves space to remember. Literally, to 're-member', to become reconnected with the person we were created to be, and reconnected to the body of humanity that was, in the beginning, created. In the beginning, God created man and woman, says the book of Genesis, and saw that they were good.

Touching the void: losing life to gain life

Why is it that many people who know they are dying – and have stopped battling to cling to life – seem to sense peace and liberation in their final days, months or even years? It is because they discover they have nothing to lose, nothing false left to attach to, and so they can live more fully within the moment. They have no future to distract them from the present, as such – so everything is focused on today. There is no pretence, no false self to complicate matters. Everything comes into perspective – into *relief*, if you like.

We need do nothing more, right now, than to notice that we all live life in the face of death (whether we like it or not). The more honest we can be about that – and about the fact that ultimately, we cannot take the spoils of our competition or consumerism or comparison with us when we go – then the more we can find ourselves liberated within the present of today.

As Ben Okri writes, 'The fear of death narrows the perspective on life; narrows it and makes all of living shrink. The fear of death makes life not worth living. It makes life a sort of living death.' [1] We simply do not want that.

Unplugging from the Matrix

The central character of the film *The Matrix*, Neo, is a loner who is searching for a mysterious character called Morpheus (named after the Greek god of dreams and sleep). He is also trying to discover the answer to the question, 'What is the Matrix?'

Morpheus contacts Neo just as the agents of the Matrix are set to stop him finding out more. 'Let me tell you why you're here,' says Morpheus. 'You're here because you know something. What you know you can't explain. But you feel it. You've felt it your entire life, that there's something wrong with the world. You don't know what it is, but it's there, like a splinter in your mind that is driving you mad...'

He continues: 'The Matrix is everywhere, it is all around us, even now in this very room. You can see it when you look out your window, or when you turn on your television. You can feel it when you go to work, when you go to church, when you pay your taxes. It is the world that has been pulled over your eyes to blind you from the truth.'

Morpheus explains that no one can be told what the Matrix really is – 'you have to see it for yourself'. And he offers Neo two pills. The red pill will answer the question 'What is the Matrix?' by removing him from it; the blue pill lets life continue as before. As Neo reaches for the red pill, Morpheus warns Neo: 'Remember, all I'm offering is the truth. Nothing more.'

Our spiritual intelligence leads us into the truth that life is not necessarily what it seems. As we begin to awaken, we have a choice to make: take the blue pill, and carry on the way we are, plugged into the same old technology, the same old distractions, the same old conspiracy to keep humans from discovering who they really are. Or we can reach for the red pill.

You are what you delete

We don't, sadly, have the stark choice of the blue pill or the red pill (I wonder which you would choose?). But there are most certainly ways of unplugging from the Matrix.

We are surrounded on every side by a world that plugs us in and refuses to let us settle into the rhythm of who we really are: adverts flash past our eyes, mobile phones keep us permanently wired, laptops, 24-hour TV, 7-days-a-week shopping...

* * *

Start to act

In order to give yourself a chance, you must give yourself space. Even for just one hour of one evening to start with, turn off the TV, unhook the phone, switch off your mobile phone, turn your mp3 player off; try to see what happens, as we thought about in

Chapter 1, when the power fails. Feel the difference. Don't be tempted to reach for a magazine – it will take you straight back into the Matrix, with its hundreds of adverts and articles for a better sex life, or how to look younger and feel better, or how to reinvent yourself for the thousandth time.

Instead, sit, and listen to the silence.

Remember, this is not about escape. It's about reconnection with life. You don't even need to escape your ego; you need to move beyond it – to transcend the exclusive domain of the mind, and move into the wholeness of who you are.

So, make yourself comfortable for however long you can cope with – 20 minutes, half an hour, an hour even… and try to sit still. Close your eyes if it helps; or focus them on a point without looking at anything specifically.

Concentrate on your breathing for a few minutes. It will help you to focus on something. Breathe in, and out. You may wish to think about breathing in goodness, or love, or God – and breathe out distraction. For the time being, simply notice what happens.

As you sit there quietly, your ego is likely to kick in; you will most probably start thinking about all the things you could be doing instead of sitting doing nothing. Don't worry or grow frustrated. Simply notice that you are thinking about these things. You might even smile to yourself – 'Here I go again' – but let your thoughts go, like the astronaut in space, without dwelling on them.

You might even like to imagine that you are standing in the room, looking at yourself sitting there. What do you see? Someone trying to settle? Someone who can't switch off? Someone who is enjoying the stillness? Notice, and then let your observation go.

Eckhart Tolle calls this process 'watching the thinker'; as you summon your 'witnessing presence', he says, you see yourself – but who is it doing the watching? Your witnessing presence is your true, your whole self, watching the thinker or the false self. You have begun the process of detachment, first by detaching from the false self of the constantly chattering mind.

Try to become aware of the sounds you wouldn't normally notice – distant cars or planes or voices or birdsong… and remain still. Breathe in, and out. Relax.

As you settle your mind down, you might also try to become more aware of the rest of your body – for this is a part of your whole self. Relax your jaw and forehead. Let your shoulders go. Feel the seat under your bottom; notice how your legs are connecting with it too. Sense the ground beneath your feet, and simply notice the connection you have physically with the world around you.

This may be the first time you have ever stopped like this to 'overhear' yourself. And I don't mean overhear your ego; you have heard that for too long. Instead, you are settling down to become aware of your real you; your deep down 'you of you'; your true self. Your embodied, communal, cooperative and incomparable self, which has been there all along, hidden.

What does it feel like? What haven't you noticed before? You are likely, quite quickly, to become aware of things you've never spotted before, details you haven't noticed. You are becoming more fully present within the room – to your self, your things, your connections – and in the process, you are moving yourself from the past and the future, where the ego resides, into the present. Try to feel the presence.

* * *

Transforming presence

Of course, we need to be aware of the past and how it has shaped us; and we need to pre-empt events in the future that we must prepare for. But that's not the same as being trapped in the past or the future, which most of us are. Most of us tend to live there, making only brief visits into the present (which are moments of awakening, if we did but recognize them). We need to reverse the process – living much more fully within the present, and making the occasional foray into past or future, as and when we need to.

The simple process of practically stopping to unplug, settle, notice the ego, become aware of your whole self, and nurture your sense of presence, is the first step towards a life of wholeness, presence, creativity, awareness, peace… It won't all come at once; it won't all come this side of eternity. But you have made a start. You have done something very profound – by doing nothing.

Playing the game of your life

Spiritual intelligence is not about getting you dressed up in orange robes and sandals, nor even about walking you through the doors of a place of worship. (You may feel inspired to find a spiritual rhythm that includes belonging to a spiritual community, of course, but I am not trying to make you do that.) Instead, this process is about drawing upon our innate spirituality to help us on the journey towards becoming more fully human.

And the journey has profoundly practical benefits. The former tennis coach and now business guru Timothy Gallwey suggests that by transcending the ego (or 'self 1' as he calls it), you can begin *practically* to flow from who you really are – whether that's on the tennis court, or in the boardroom, or the bedroom, or wherever.

And he starts very, very simply. Our minds, he suggests, overcomplicate things for us. When we are not thinking about how to do something, we tend to do it well, and naturally – like walking, for example. There are innumerable things our body needs to do in order to perform the act of walking, but we do it effortlessly. It's when we really think about things that we tend to tense up.

You may have experienced this when playing sport. If you're having a simple knockabout on the tennis court, and you're not attached to winning, then you're likely to play some nice, flowing shots, very naturally. Put yourself into a formal game, however, and if you're competitive (or worried about being shown up!) then that voice in your head will kick in faster than you can say 'Deuce!' Concentrate, it will say. You can't afford to lose this, you idiot. Throw the ball higher. Hit it harder. Don't put it into the net…

And of course, you put it into the net. Self 1 talks you into fluffing it.

Gallwey says that you can learn to catch a ball (if you don't know how to!) simply by transcending self 1. He has taught many people, in a remarkable way at his workshops, to catch. First, he throws them a ball to show that they can't catch it. Then, in the following throws, he begins to ask them what they notice about the ball itself. And as they raise their awareness, and shut out the mind that is trying to tell them *how* to catch it, they catch it. Most people, he says, go from catching it two times out of ten to catching it eight times instead.

It's as simple as that. And as with catching a ball, so with life. As you learn to transcend the ego, detach from your fears of dropping the ball (literally or metaphorically), and become aware instead of the world around you, you begin to flow from your true self, and play the game of your life.

Raising awareness

As you practise the art of detaching, simply by spending more time in quiet reflection and contemplation, you should begin to notice practical results: you will feel reconnected with the world around you; you will notice small details and sometimes colours will seem more vivid; you will rediscover creativity and find ideas welling up from unexpected places, out of the blue; you will remain calm under pressure, and not get entangled in emotional or political turmoil; you'll keep your head when all around you people are losing theirs, by remembering that your head is part of a greater, whole self! And your own, embodied presence will begin to have a positive, peaceful, inspiring effect on those around you (more of which in the next chapter).

Noticing the false self of the Other, and detaching from it

Here's something else you will begin to notice: as you become aware of your ego and how to detach from it, you are also more likely to become aware of other egos at work. You can use this in one of two ways. Negatively, you might feel tempted to begin to judge others as you notice how they cling to their attachments. Don't: that's your own, judgmental ego kicking in again. Never look for the speck in someone else's eye when you have a plank in yours.

Instead, see past the other person's ego to who they really are – their undiscovered true self – and learn to love them for it. And if their ego attacks you, or unsettles you, do not engage with it – because again, as you do, your ego is likely to engage.

Instead, when you find yourself caught in an argument, let it go. Detach. Notice your pride or your hurt and smile gently and let it go. Nothing can damage your true self, your witnessing presence, because it has nothing to lose. It owns nothing; it is attached to nothing; it is a part of everything – the wholeness of Life.

Ultimately, and this will take much practice, you will learn naturally to let your inner depths call to the inner depths of others, instead of locking horns like rutting deer with other egos. Begin to become aware of this at a business meeting or in any potentially stressful situation you are about to encounter. As you access your own deep, incomparable self, you will find the confidence to let any 'egoic' attacks pass, and to engage soulfully and with great presence of mind with others, without becoming emotional.

Drop your weapons

You may feel, at this point, that all this sounds a little too much like surrender for your liking. Well, on one level, it *is* complete surrender. You are beginning to surrender all that the ego has held onto so tightly for so long. Drop your weapons of attack and defence, and walk away: although you have been fighting this battle all of your life, it is *not* the one you were created to fight. The challenge ahead is to pick your battles more carefully.

As you nurture your spiritual intelligence, you will begin to notice that there is a different battle altogether that you are called to fight. It is a battle for your own heart, and for the hearts of those around you. It is a battle against injustice, on behalf of those who need you most. It is a battle for soul.

This is not some feeble spiritual surrender. As you surrender the things in life you've believed are the most important, you will begin to realize they were the least important all along. And you will be freed to begin the fight of your life: the fight for what is right.

If you only seek to serve yourself and your own ego, you will, in the end, lose the battle. Great leaders need a great cause to lead. It is by discovering the noble art of battling for others in the great cause of life that you will begin to find your calling. All else is mere illusion.

Incomparable acts of beauty

Remember, we are concerned about the Way we are seeking to travel: we are interested in today, in the small decisions and the myriad choices we make, moment by moment, within the great expanse of the present.

We cannot grasp beauty; yet when we let it go, we allow it to flow through us and out towards others. And as it does so, as we channel it and let it go, it becomes a beauty that is unique to us. As we marry action with contemplation – doing with being – and as we begin to pass on that which we receive, we start to become the change we want to see.

Think of yourself not as a consumer, but as a 'co-creator' with life; of small, sustainable acts of beauty, which are not yours to hold on to, but which flow like a river of life to those around you.

The things you have attached to, in order to create a shell of beauty for your self, will fade away. As the depths of God call to your inner depths, and as you, in turn, call to the inner depths in others, you will begin to live a life of incomparable beauty. One step at a time.

But for now, take your time. Breathe deeply. Relax. You're going on a journey.

Chapter 8

Passing it on

To be a person is to have a story to tell.
Isak Dinesen

We are almost through level 2, and you have now been introduced to the idea of becoming aware of, and 'detaching' from, your ego or false self. The question now is, how are the benefits passed on to those around you – your family, or team, or company, or community?

Imagine you were the daughter or son of Bill Gates, but no one knew; and imagine you were doing your usual job. Your inheritance would be absolutely secure because of your relationship with your father, so you would have nothing to lose by being yourself – you would not have to pretend to be somehow better than you are, or someone different to who you are. The chances are, you would approach a high-pressure meeting with your boss or with an important client in quite a different, liberating way.

But you don't have to be related to a multi-billionaire to live a life of freedom. Remove your attachments – to success, or proving your worth, or winning the deal – and you also begin to remove fear: fear of the other person, or of being shown up, or losing a contract, or being passed over for promotion.

Perhaps you would feel more relaxed. Perhaps you would feel as if you didn't want to pretend you could offer something you really know you couldn't – because ultimately, you didn't need to. Perhaps you would be more honest. Perhaps you would have greater presence of mind. Perhaps you would see the other person as a human being, and not as a client or as competition. Perhaps you would feel more creative, sharper. Perhaps you would feel as if you need to perform less, and be yourself more. Perhaps you would begin to really enjoy yourself. And perhaps other people would begin to enjoy you, as someone who truly stands out from the crowd, who is assured yet humble, effective without being driven, committed yet not clinging, offering an invitation, not trying to persuade or sell.

If only life were really like that. If only we could detach from the voice in our head that is driving us to prove ourselves to whoever is watching. If only we could remove the fear and live from our true self, so that our presence could lift a room, issue a challenge for justice, provide a creative alternative, or model a different way of being.

What's stopping you?

* * *

Stop to think
What *is* stopping you?

* * *

Most of don't live to our full potential, as the people we were created to be, because we rarely experience what it is to *be* that person. We spend so much of our time *doing* things that we end up defining ourselves by what we do and what we try to achieve, instead of by who we are.

Being and doing are inseparable; you are not to forget your 'doing', but to reconnect it with a heightened awareness of your 'being'. If you manage that, then you will begin to bring the person you really are to those meetings at work, to your family, to your friends, to your community.

So who *are* you? We have already begun to stop, to do nothing, in order to 'overhear' ourselves and reconnect with the greater whole of who we are. But in this chapter we will think about the story in which we find ourselves – as a way of reflecting further on who we are, and what we can do as a result.

'I wonder what sort of tale we've fallen into'

A little way into the *Lord of the Rings* trilogy (by J. R. R. Tolkien), the hobbits Frodo and Samwise (who have set out on an epic journey to dispose of the powerful, seductive Ring) are beset with dangers and enemies on every side. Having enjoyed a quiet, uneventful life in the Shire, they now find themselves on a terrifying adventure. They don't fully know it yet, but the future of Middle Earth rests upon their commitment, courage and resolve to keep going.

Little Samwise, a very ordinary and unremarkable hobbit, is reflecting on the adventure that they seem to have landed in. 'I used to think that [adventures] were things the wonderful folk of the stories went out and looked for, because they wanted them, because they were exciting and life was a bit dull, a kind of a sport, as you might say. But that's not the way of it with the tales that really mattered, or the ones that stay in the mind. Folk seem to have been just landed in them, usually – their paths were laid that way, as you put it. But I expect they had lots of chances, like us, of turning back, only they didn't...

'I wonder what kind of tale we've fallen into.'

It's a question we all need to ask. Because without it, we have little or no sense of purpose or direction, little reason to keep going, little understanding of how we can bring who we are to the people we are travelling with, in pursuit of a common goal.

* * *

Stop to think
What kind of story have you fallen into?

* * *

Why is it that the really great adventure stories, such as *Lord of the Rings*, or *The Matrix*, or *Star Wars*, or the great love stories like *Gone with the Wind* or *Titanic* move us deep in our guts, in an often visceral way? It's because they reflect somehow a bigger story that is unfolding around us; they help us (as we identify with the characters) to see how the little story of our own lives connects with something much bigger – and that we may have a role to play within that bigger story.

As the novelist Ben Okri writes, 'The greatest stories are those that resonate our beginnings and intuit our endings, our mysterious origins and our numinous destinies, and dissolve them both into one.'[1] They help us to know where we've come from and where we're going, so that we understand more about who we are now.

The author Eugene Peterson wrote: 'Story doesn't just tell us something and leave it there, it invites our participation.'[2]

And the writer Daniel Taylor says, 'You "are" your stories. You are the product of all the stories you have heard and lived – and of many that you have never heard. They have shaped how you see yourself, the world, and your place in it.'[3]

In other words, story matters, big time. Yet the novelist Douglas Coupland writes that we have lost our sense of story. In today's consumer culture, we have become, in his words, 'de-narrated' – and 'de-narrated', for him, means 'not having a life'. We have lost a sense of where we have come from, where we are heading and, as a consequence, who we are right now. We need to get a life. We need to get a story.

* * *

Stop to think
What is your favourite story, or film, or play, or song lyric...? Why? What does it say about you?

How does your favourite story help to set the story of your own life in context?

* * *

Three unfolding storylines

You might find it helpful to think of three unfolding storylines in your life: your own personal story ('me'); the communal story of you and those around you ('we'); and the global or cosmic story of which everyone and everything is a part ('the Bigger Picture').

The three need to flow meaningfully into each other.

When we become 'de-narrated', as Coupland suggests, we lose sense of how our own story fits with the Bigger Picture. We feel powerless to shape events in the wider world – they're things that simply happen to us, *end of story* – and so we become passive, taking what we can from the world around us, without thinking about what can give. Unable to demonstrate any strong sense of purpose to our lives, we feel disconnected both from the Bigger Picture and from the story of those around us. We become atomized.

Those rare people who know and can demonstrate how their own story flows meaningfully into the unfolding Bigger Picture are remarkable, quite literally: they stand out, because they have searched their hearts and discovered their true self, their passion and their vision, and they have a higher cause to serve. They are able to show how their own story makes sense within the Bigger Picture, and how their life can make a difference within it. They believe they are able to shape the Bigger Picture that's emerging by serving it and giving themselves and their life to it, thus demonstrating strong qualities of natural leadership – and turning the story of 'I' into the story of 'we' in the process.

As the Oscar-winning screenwriter Ron Bass wrote, 'When I pitch a story, I have to sell myself – who I am. The same is true of every leader, in business or any other field. Take Barack Obama. His story is all about who he is. And everything about him is part of it, down to his physical presence: the eye contact, the hand on the shoulder, the sound of his voice.'[4]

We may not all be Barack Obama, but we do all have a story to tell, and deep down, we probably sense that it should contribute to something beyond our own egoistic desires. For if our story is simply about ourselves, it will ultimately alienate those around us.

Bringing benefits to others through shaping the story of 'we'

'Even in today's cynical, self-centred age, people are desperate to believe in something bigger than themselves,' writes Peter Gruber in the *Harvard Business Review*. 'The storyteller plays a vital role by providing them with a mission they can believe in and devote themselves to.'[5]

So what *is* your story? Have you stopped to think?

As we begin to think about 'life as story', it provides us with a way of seeing that our own story must transcend our ego, to reach out to, connect with and bring meaning to those around us. Ultimately, if you begin to reflect upon and express your own story powerfully, you will help others to find meaning for themselves if you can show

how they might connect with something bigger, beyond themselves. And thus, in 'passing it on' – in learning to tell your story both in word and actions – you will bring benefit to others.

* * *

Start to act

1. *The story you have received in life*

Spend some time writing or noting or contemplating the story you have received in life: the script you've been expected to live up to. You might recall words your parents or teachers have spoken that have had a bearing on your life, negatively or positively. Think of the circumstances you were born into (your location, class, prospects…). Think of the people who were part of the 'plot'. Think of the wounds you received, as well as the good things that happened to you. What is the story you received from the external forces in your life? How has it affected or captivated you?

2. *The Bigger Picture of which you are a part*

Once you've done that, consider the Bigger Picture in which you are living, and identify which parts of the Bigger Picture are really relevant to you and your story. Elements of the Bigger Picture may include God, the global economy, climate change, the state of your nation, poverty and injustice, war, the company you work for, the postmodern world, human nature, human history… You may think of others. Which elements specifically do you either feel connected to, or oppressed by, or helpless in the face of? Which interest you the most? Try to write a short account of the Bigger Picture.

3. *The story you'd like to leave behind*

Now think about the episodes of the story you have received that you would like to transform or rewrite for good. Which events would you like to leave behind? Which hurtful words would you like to let go of? Which forces beyond your control would you like to extricate yourself from? What are the points of departure for you as you begin a new journey of discovery and adventure?

4. Key transformational moments in your life

Next, consider those moments in your life that have provided crucial, positive turning points (even if they felt negative at the time). What were they? What happened? What did you learn about yourself through them? How could they contribute to the sense of an unfolding, positive plot-line in your life? For each moment, try to write a paragraph or two, and think of a visual image or symbol that might illustrate each point. You may perhaps identify five or six key moments that have been pivotal, and five or six images to go with them.

5. Characters within the story

Who has been an important influence in your life? Who are you disconnected from whom you need to reconnect with? Who would you like to be a part of your future story? Write down their names, and think of how you hope to serve these people, as well as receive from them.

6. The story you would like to tell (and live)

Now, begin to assemble your key moments from the past, as well as any aspirations you have for the future. But crucially, ask yourself how these can link to the Bigger Picture you identified earlier. What is the cause you would like to serve through your life? How can you give your whole self to it? How can you connect to elements in the Bigger Picture through who you are and what you do? How can your story become about more than just you? How would you like your story to unfold so that it demonstrates to others the way *they* can find meaning and purpose within the present? Write a narrative about where you've come from and where you believe you're heading, and why this brings meaning and purpose to who you are and what you're doing now.

7. Think of your audience

Who would most benefit from hearing a purposeful story of your life? Who would find it helpful or inspiring? Who would benefit from the way you are being transformed? (The people around you? The poor or oppressed? Your clients? Your 'neighbours'?) How would you tailor your story for your particular audience?

8. Check yourself for integrity

Ask yourself what story these people, in turn, would tell about you. How would it differ from the one you wish to tell? How can you help the story they tell about you to become integrated with the story you tell about yourself, so that your story has power and integrity and can draw others in?

9. Begin to tell your new story, and ask for feedback

Remember that your story will be at its most powerful when you are able to demonstrate how your own story makes sense within the Bigger Picture. Keep asking yourself how, by telling your story, you can help others to begin to tell and live a meaningful story for themselves.

10. What is the communal story (the story of 'we') that you would like to nurture through your immediate relationships?

This may be something very specific: it may be the story of your team or department at work, or your book group, or your family or marriage or friendship group. Who is involved in this story? How can they find their voice within it? How can you help lead the way, by serving these people with ego-less, self-giving service?

* * *

It's little wonder that businesses are increasingly awakening to the power of story, and to the need to help their employees to rediscover a sense of meaning in their working lives and reconnect with a higher purpose. 'Stories are the single most powerful weapon in a leader's arsenal,' writes Howard Gardner of Harvard University. If businesses are on to it, you can usually bet there's a good reason to pay attention.

But don't focus on developing your story for selfish reasons, or for personal gain. Instead, stay true to the idea of 'passing it on', as we come to the end of the second level of the iconic journey. For this is about helping you to transcend your ego, discovering the whole, incomparable you, and beginning to pass on the benefits to those around you *through your journey of discovery*.

There is one last thing to say about story, for now. We have focused specifically on reflecting upon, and expressing, your own story. But crucially, we also need to become active, curious listeners to the stories of others.

The author and poet Maya Angelou said, 'There is no agony like bearing an untold story inside of you.' And she is most certainly right. Perhaps you have never been asked to tell your story. Perhaps no one has ever shown an interest. It's quite likely. And so it's also quite likely that you haven't asked the people around you to tell you theirs (especially the ones who are least forthcoming).

A little knowledge about someone can be a dangerous thing. You may think you know them, simply because you have 'known' them for a long time. But have you actually asked them to tell you their *story*? If not, do. You will almost certainly be surprised by what you hear, and how little you really knew.

And as you listen, consider it a sacred act. Something very special happens when you allow another person the space and opportunity to truly tell their story. You create a covenant between teller and listener. This is extraordinarily unusual and powerful. As you focus your attention on another person and honour their story, you honour their very being.

God knows, every story counts. And at this bewildering time in our human history, we need to rediscover the art of telling a great story about life, through life.

The true self

Chapter 9

Awakening

Your dead shall live; their bodies shall rise. You who dwell in the dust, awake and sing for joy! For your dew is a dew of light, and the earth will give birth to the dead.
Isaiah 26:19

So we come to the start of level 3; and this is where we (hopefully) begin to find ourselves. It is time to awaken to the possibilities of who we really are; of who we have always been, below the surface, if we did but know it. And certainly, of who we can become as we move forward.

It is one thing to identify the person we are not; that is a difficult, but manageable task, especially because it's not so hard to recognize the constant chattering of the ego-driven mind once it's been pointed out to us. But it requires patience and faith and courage now to begin to awaken to the person we were created to be in the first place.

* * *

Stop to think
We all go through times of transformation, though it's not always easy to spot them when they're happening to us. Sometimes, it's only when we've been through them that we see how much we've really changed. When I began running, I also began to lose weight. I probably lost around two stone (12 kg) over the course of a year. But it was only when someone commented to me, 'You've lost weight!', that I realized I'd undergone real change. I had been focused on the task of getting out there, day in, day out, to run; the happy consequence was that I was looking a lot better for it.

In the last chapter, I asked you to reflect upon your story, and within that, to identify some key times in which you'd experienced change or transformation. Think of one of those times now, and ask yourself how you changed. When did you notice that things had become different, somehow? How might you describe the nature of the change you underwent? Was it positive, or less so? Can you remember how people around you reacted to what was happening to you? How might they have been changed, as a result?

Think of a metaphor for change, and apply it to yourself. You might return to the metaphor of a journey, to continue reflecting on how far you've come, and what's happening to you right now. Alternatively, you might reflect on something transformative – such as a caterpillar turning into a butterfly, or a seed turning into a plant. Each has to undergo a profound 'death' in its original form, in order to realize its full, incomparable potential.

How might you describe your experience, as you consider 'dying' to your incomplete, ego-driven self, and start living instead with the wholeness of who you really are? Can you think of a metaphor or symbol that would help you to contemplate who you are, and who you are becoming?

* * *

As we reflect upon what it means to *awaken* to our true self, let's remember an important truth within this process: that we must *want* to be healed, and we must want to desire to relinquish those attachments that skew our true sense of identity.

As William P. Young, author of the tremendously popular novel *The Shack*, suggests, it's too easy to keep hanging on to unhelpful things, even when we've begun to glimpse the possibilities of something better. 'People are tenacious when it comes to the treasure of their imaginary independence,' he writes. 'They hoard and hold their sickness with a firm grip. They find their identity and worth in their brokenness and guard it with every ounce of strength they have. No wonder grace has such little attraction. You have tried to lock the door of your heart from the inside.'[1]

It's not unlike when Jesus confronts a man who has been sitting for years and years beside a healing pool, the 'pool of Siloam'. According to John's Gospel, legend had it that an angel would stir up the waters of the pool, and that when this happened, the first person into the pool would be healed.

Jesus asked the man, 'Do you *want* to be healed?' It seems like an outrageous question, to begin with. Of course he does. Doesn't he? He's been sitting there waiting for this healing opportunity for much of his life. And yet Jesus knows that you must *want* to be healed, in order to receive the healing. It can't be forced upon you. Sometimes, you can become too used to your state of brokenness.

Here, then, we arrive at a crossroads, a place at which we sense we can be healed and move into a whole, new way of being. The question is, are we willing to embrace such healing, and move on? Are you willing to surrender the identity that you have created out of your wounds and insecurities and deficiencies?

Remember that, for now, in this chapter, we are simply talking about awakening. Your task is to do little more than *notice*. Do you wish to leave behind the trappings of identity created by a mind that has been acting defensively and offensively on your behalf? Notice how you feel when confronted with this question. It may be that you need to awaken most profoundly, for now, to the idea that you may not wish to enter a deeper realm of wholeness, for a whole number of reasons.

* * *

Start to act
Spend some silent, extended reflection on this very question: Do you want to be healed? Are you prepared to encounter the rest of who you are – the whole you, which has been buried for so long?

* * *

Sensing the glow

*The realization of the call of God in a person's life may come with
a sudden thunder clap or by a gradual dawning, but in whatever
way it comes, it comes with the under-current of the supernatural,
almost the uncanny. It is always accompanied with a glow –*

*something that cannot be put into words. We need to keep the
atmosphere of our mind prepared by the Holy Spirit lest we forget
the surprise of the touch of God on our lives.*
Oswald Chambers[2]

It's not always easy to let go and experience the new. Sometimes,
you simply have to be willing to give it a try. It is an act of faith.
But imagine, for a moment, that you were indeed created by a
loving God; if that's true (and you may believe it, or you may be
thinking about it), then you have nothing to lose but your own
false expectations and fears and attachments. Unless a seed falls to
the ground and dies, it will not grow.

Eckhart Tolle is convinced by the positive effects of awakening
to the whole you. 'The moment you start watching the thinker,' he
suggests, 'a higher level of consciousness becomes activated. You
begin to realise that there is a vast realm of intelligence beyond
thought, that thought is only a tiny aspect of that intelligence.
You also realise that all the things that truly matter – beauty, love,
creativity, joy, inner peace – arise from beyond the mind. *You begin
to awaken.*'[3]

It's perhaps like waking from a long sleep, and switching on a light.
You can't necessarily open your eyes wide straight away. They must
become accustomed to the light. Nevertheless, you can sense the
light; it's a new day, with new possibilities: and when the possibilities
involve discovering 'beauty, love, creativity, joy, inner peace...', then
it's surely worth not rolling over and going back to sleep.

* * *

Stop to think
Oswald Chambers talks of 'the call of God' on your life. What do
you think he means by 'the call'? How might you have experienced
a call from God? Have you ever felt drawn – compelled perhaps –
to follow a certain path in your life, or to make a certain decision?
Have you sensed the presence of God? If so, where? How would
you describe the creative tension between overhearing your
whole, true self, and overhearing 'the call' of God from outside
of yourself? Is there a difference? Why do you think it is that the
quieter we become, and the more we detach from our ego, the

easier it might be to hear the voice of God as well as the voice within our heart?

* * *

And God saw that it was good

One of the most crucial things we can awaken to in this whole process is the battle between good and evil, and how we can become caught in the crossfire. It's a battle between the incomplete self and the whole or true self, between the people we were originally created to be and the people we've ended up being. And we must enter the battle daily. We are learning to become spiritual warriors because we are awakening to a cause worth fighting for.

Of course, this battle has been played out in many works of art and fiction through the years. Think of *Dr Jeckyl and Mr Hyde*, and any number of cartoon characters pictured with an angel on one shoulder and a devil on the other...

It is very hard not to think badly of 'human nature', because of what has happened to the human race throughout history. We have just brought to a close the bloodiest century in human history, the twentieth. And it's not just on a global scale that we struggle.

You might catch yourself saying with alarming regularity, 'I can't help it: *I'm only human.*' We use it as an excuse, though we tend to believe that we really *are* only human, and that being human means being at a disadvantage. Of course, as humans, we have weaknesses and we stumble and fall constantly. That's part of the deal. But we tend to focus on these weaknesses, if we are not careful, and fail, in the process, to see the mark of the Creator on our humanity.

That's why we thought in the very first chapter about the person we might see staring back at us when we look in the mirror in the morning when we wake up and brush our teeth. It's so easy not to like what you see. So many of us look at our reflection and wish we were different, somehow – younger, prettier, more vivacious or curvaceous...

And so many of us avoid any deeper kind of reflection – such as meditation or contemplation – because we are afraid that, just like staring into the mirror, we won't like what we see staring back at us, upon reflection.

But what if the reflection were much better than we'd expected? What if, like Cinderella, we had it in us to be a princess all along? We may have been dressed in rags and neglected, but we were destined to be royal, beautiful, honoured. What if, like Quasimodo, we were a prince trapped in the body of an ogre?

The book of Genesis tells a story of that mysterious time when the world was breathed into being. The musician Moby once produced a lovely piano track called 'God Moving Over the Face of the Waters'. It is like a pregnant pause, a work of mystery, capturing that moment before creation was born.

Some people take the Genesis account of creation literally; many others believe that it contains ancient wisdom about our beginnings, expressed in the form of story. Whatever you think of this text, theologians have highlighted that it contains a radical, revolutionary thought that we have, over time, come to almost ignore: that God created us, and God saw that we were 'good'.

He was pleased with his creation. And we were born with what some theologians call 'original blessing'; born with the imprint of the Creator, who said, 'Let us make [humanity] in our own image.'

It was only subsequently that we fell from grace, somehow. The book of Genesis talks of Adam and Eve being tempted by the serpent in the Garden of Eden. The story goes that they ate the forbidden fruit from the Tree of the Knowledge of Good and Evil, realized they were naked, felt ashamed, and hid from God. However we interpret this, most of us acknowledge that we do, indeed, live within a fallen state of grace. In fact, it's been hammered home to us ever since, by news readers and preachers and artists and commentators. We know that something has gone badly wrong. Christians call it 'original sin' – meaning that we are all born sinful – but we tend, within our brokenness, to forget that originally, we were created good, and that humanity itself was born with original blessing.

As we try to slow down and shut out the background noise of a culture stuck on fast forward, as we practise contemplation, dwell within silence, and switch off the ever-working ego-driven mind, we offer ourselves the chance to remember not just who we were created to be, as individuals, but who we were created to be as humanity. And as we do so, something very deep within us stretches out to be reconnected with that original state of blessing.

We long to return to the Garden.

* * *

Stop to think
What do you think it was like in those first, great days of Creation? What was it was like to be in an unbroken relationship with other people, with God, and with the Creation in which God has placed us? What do you miss about those times? What is it, do you sense, that the deepest part of you longs to be 're-connected' to, 're-membered'?

* * *

Perhaps you miss having nothing to prove. Perhaps you miss relaxing in the knowledge that you are really someone. Perhaps you miss knowing the Creator who brought you into being. Perhaps you miss that deepest sense of belonging. Perhaps you miss peace.

Of course, nothing this side of eternity will make us completely whole. We live to the 'East of Eden', as fragmented, broken people, caught in a struggle. We literally talk about 'falling apart' or 'cracking up'; if we did but know it, we sense our lack of wholeness very keenly.

But we are not to despair. For the journey back to wholeness does not happen when we or if we make it to heaven. It starts now. And it starts by awakening to the idea that we were created 'good', as children of God.

* * *

Stop to think
Sometimes it takes other people to point out the beauty of who we really are. We tend to tell a story about ourselves, *to* ourselves, that is most probably not positive (whether that's the story we tell others or not; often it is not). Sometimes we are taken aback by a positive word of encouragement, even if such words are rare. Sometimes, others can see a beauty within you that may be hidden

from your own sight. Think back to a time when someone gave you some disarmingly positive feedback. Don't let that recollection feed your ego; instead, receive that affirmation afresh. Listen to it. Remind yourself of it. You're not all bad, after all. In fact, there is much within you that is good.

* * *

If you find this hard to do, think about someone you know, and apply it to them, for a moment. Sometimes it is easier to see the good in others. Think of your friends or work colleagues. Of course, they have their foibles; they are, after all, mostly operating from the realm of the ego-driven mind, and so they will have their own titanic struggles to contend with. But you can probably see through their ego, past their insecurities and idiosyncrasies, towards glimpses of the real 'them'.

* * *

Start to act
Think specifically of one person you know quite well. You may wish to notice immediately your reaction to that person, which may be a complex jumble of judgmentalism and affection. Try to identify or overhear your ego judging their faults, and let this pass. Let your critique of that person go.

Now, consider what it is that's beautiful about that person. Think what it is, about them, that inspires goodness within you. What is it about their 'deep' that calls to your 'deep', and how does that help to transform you? What is it about the way that person acts, speaks, works, lives, that you aspire to emulate? Why do you truly appreciate them? What might you say about them at their wedding or funeral or in a leaving speech?

Now, try to think what they might specifically appreciate about you in the same way. If you are truly daring, you might even raise the subject (using this book as a prompt or an excuse) with them, and take the opportunity to express the story you tell about each other.

* * *

When working with companies or organizations, my colleagues at MCA and I have used something called 'the greatness exercise' to help people awaken to what is really 'great' (in the true sense) about them. Usually, this has happened over a drink at the bar after a day's workshop, to help them relax and loosen up a little. It can be hard to talk openly about such things (though the spiritually intelligent person will do so without the aid of a drink!).

Each person is asked to write down how each of the others is 'great in my eyes'. We then go around the group taking each person in turn. Everyone explains why they appreciate that one particular person – why they are great – while someone else records the comments for them. Almost always, the experience is profoundly moving, and it frequently produces tears. Some people have never heard a work colleague say anything positive about them before, and frequently you hear people saying, 'I had no idea you thought that about me.' If only we took the trouble to tell each other such things without prompt, or at times other than at workshops or weddings or funerals.

But we all bear the image of greatness because we are made in the image of a great God. We still need to repent, as we thought about in Chapter 7, detaching from unhelpful or uncaring judgments and behaviours that are manifested when we defend ourselves and attack others through our ego-driven 'self'; but that is part of our transformation. As we repent, and 'die' to our incomplete, false self, we begin to awaken to the whole, true self we were created to be. And that self is very good.

Chapter 10

Seeing afresh

At core, our new world view involves seeing yourself, others, and all of life, not through the eyes of the our small, earthly self that lives in time and is born in time. But rather through the eyes of the soul, our Being, the True Self.
Russell E. DiCarlo[1]

This is one of the miracles of love: It gives a power of seeing through its own enchantments and yet not being disenchanted.
C. S. Lewis[2]

Your eyes are windows into your body. If you open your eyes wide in wonder and belief, your body fills up with light. If you live squinty-eyed in greed and distrust, your body is a dank cellar. If you pull the blinds on your windows, what a dark life you will have!
Matthew 6:22

And so now, we continue the journey into an even deeper way of seeing. We have already stopped to ask how we see ourselves and the world around us, and have begun to try to notice *how* we see it, and how we might see it differently. And we have thought about how it's unhelpful to see with the eyes of the mind alone, from the perspective of the ego-driven self. Now, it's time to think more carefully about the beauty and potential that we might see – in ourselves, in each other, in the world in which we live, and in God – as we begin to look from another place within us, our soul.

Let's remember that our task is to marry our doing with our being. With the first two icons of each journey – awakening and seeing afresh – we are a little more focused on our being: stopping to notice, to see and hear and taste and touch life in a different way. Yet all the while, we are travelling purposefully through our doing as well; towards a whole, new way of being, in which what we do flows from who we are – seeking integration, well-being and wholeness in ourselves and others, through nurturing our spiritual intelligence.

* * *

Transformation means seeing afresh

The art of seeing has always captured the imagination of those with spiritual intelligence. You may not know of the story of Saul of Tarsus, but most of us have heard of the phrase, 'a Damascus-road experience'. Saul was an enemy of the Jews who had converted to Christianity in the earliest days of the church. As he travelled to Damascus to aid in the mortal persecution of these new believers, he was blinded by a light from heaven, fell from his horse, heard a voice and lost his sight. When he recovered his vision three days later, he was transformed; 'scales fell from his eyes' and he became a passionate believer in a new cause.[3] His own transformation was intrinsically caught up in 'seeing afresh'.

He began to see himself, others, the world around him, in a different way; and this *way* of seeing fundamentally changed not just his outlook but his identity. He changed his name to Paul as a result.

Few of us have a 'Damascus-road' experience with quite such dramatic, undeniable effect; in fact, most of us would probably identify more closely with another saying of Paul's, that 'we see through a glass, darkly' – in other words, that we have to admit with humility that we don't fully understand everything this side of eternity. Nevertheless, it is crucial that we seek not just to see, but to perceive, even when all is not clear; and to notice both *what* we see, and *how* we see it.

* * *

Stop to think

Has there ever been a time in your life when 'the scales fell from your eyes' – when your eyes were opened to someone or something and you began to see in a different way? Think of a person you judged negatively before you had even spoken to them – someone who you came to realize was very different from your initial perception of them. What is the difference between the way you *saw* that person before, and the way you *see* them now?

In defensive mode (which is where the ego operates from), we tend to look for things we can 'judge' about other people or situations. We search rapidly for things on the surface that may bolster our fears or prejudices and create an impression in our mind that we can use to defend ourselves or attack the other. How can you see people in a different way? What are the scales that must fall from your eyes?

* * *

Seeing eye-to-eye

We have already thought about the way we each see the world uniquely. That is a God-given gift. Yet we must beware of using such a gift simply as a way of getting ahead or, perhaps worse, of trying to persuade everyone else to see things from our own perspective. In fact, the spiritually intelligent approach to seeing is to begin to see things from the perspective of others. It doesn't always matter if we don't see eye-to-eye, as long as we try to see through the eyes of the Other.

* * *

This is water

As we stop to 'notice', we become more fully aware and awake. And awareness and wakefulness shape our actions. We 'are', and then we 'do'. As we notice more, we become more aware of the way we see the world, and of the world view we have grown up with or have bought into. We may notice, for example, that we have grown up within capitalism, and that it is a system, not simply 'the way things are' or have always been. We may notice that we have a 'default setting', a way of seeing the world that we've been brought up to believe is 'normal'. And we may begin to notice that things don't always have to be that way; and that we don't always have to see the world in the way that the predominant culture does.

But even if we have glimpsed a greater truth and have begun to see things in a different light, we can forget so quickly and move back to our default setting, especially when the pressure is on. One of our greatest tasks in life is to choose to see things differently, day by day, hour by hour. To be wakeful to the reality of the world around us.

The great contemporary novelist David Foster Wallace gave a commencement speech for graduates at Kenyon College, Ohio. 'There are these two young fish swimming along,' he said, 'and they happen to meet an older fish swimming the other way, who nods at them and says, "Morning, boys, how's the water?" And the two young fish swim on for a bit, and then eventually one of them looks over at the other and goes, "What the hell is water?"'

He explains, 'The immediate point is that the most obvious, ubiquitous important realities are often the ones that are the hardest to see and talk about.'

We often have a choice about the way we see things around us; it's just that we tend automatically to see things as we have been programmed or conditioned to see them. And that's usually from the perspective of the ego – from our own narrow, limiting perspective – and so we interpret them as such.

Wallace argues that it's in precisely the kind of mundane, annoying, stultifying situations that vex us most – such as food-shopping – that you can and need to choose to see things differently. It's in these moments that we can decide to journey towards wholeness. The whole of life matters, remember. Life is holy, and every moment precious.

Picture the scene: 'You finally get to the checkout line's front, and pay for your food,' he writes, 'and wait to get your cheque or card authenticated by a machine, and then get told to "Have a nice day" in a voice that is the absolute voice of death, and then you have to take your creepy flimsy plastic bags of groceries in your cart through the bumpy, littery parking lot, and try to load the bags in your car in such a way that everything doesn't fall out of the bags and roll around in the trunk, and then you have to drive all the way home through slow, heavy, SUV-intensive rush-hour traffic...'

Potentially, it's a nightmare; yet this is where the act of choosing really comes in. 'Because the traffic jams and crowded aisles and long checkout lines give me time to think, and if I don't make a conscious decision about how to think and what to pay attention to, I'm going to be pissed and miserable every time I have to food-shop...'

He has a point. How much time do we waste wishing we were somewhere else, being dragged down by the way we see things unfolding around us?

If you've begun to learn how to 'pay attention', however – and have noticed that there are other perspectives from which you can choose to see what's going on – then you will have other options. You can notice the humanity of the people, for a start. And you can notice that not everything revolves around you. You can become aware of how your own presence within such a situation can lift and transform the experience of others, too – such as the lady on the checkout we usually ignore.

'It will be within your power to experience a crowded, loud, slow, consumer-hell-type situation as not only meaningful but sacred, on fire with the same force that lit the stars – compassion, love, the sub-surface unity of all things. Not that that mystical stuff's necessarily true: the only thing that's capital-True is that you get to decide how you're going to try to *see* it.

'You get to consciously decide what has meaning and what doesn't. You get to decide what to worship,' he concludes.

In choosing how we see the world around us, we also begin to change what we see. And therein lies a mystery.

* * *

Start to act

Next time you are stuck in a traffic jam, notice how you react. It's quite possible that your mind is so intent on reaching your destination that you very quickly begin to feel dissatisfied, cross, frustrated; any sense of 'presence' you have – of being present within the moment – may evaporate, as you stretch forward, wishing you were able to move on at speed. And yet you are powerless to act; so why spend the time you have getting more and more stressed?

As you notice how you are feeling, try to smile gently with your witnessing presence at your ego, and let your ego-driven thoughts subside. Be still. Breathe deeply, and become aware of your breathing. And try to become fully present to the moment. Become aware of your body, whether it is tense or relaxed. Feel the connection between the chair and your legs. Sense the connection between you and the other drivers around you. Notice things you may not normally notice – the surface of the road, perhaps, or simply what it feels like to be sitting still with hundreds of other people, not going anywhere. (Where else do you get to savour such an experience?!) You have a choice: to dwell within this present moment, alive to yourself and those around you, or to wish you weren't there. One way will bring peace, joy, contentment, stillness, meditation, wholeness, thanks to the utterly mundane experience; the other will transport you instantly to a place of stress and turmoil. One, you live from the true self; the other, from the false. You can choose.

* * *

There are many things to see differently if you begin to choose to do so. But let's reflect on four areas of relationship: we can choose to see ourselves, each other, the planet and God differently, if we continue to become more fully aware of who we really are within such an intricate, beautiful web of life.

Seeing yourself through fresh eyes

'The ego self is the unobserved self,' writes Father Richard Rohr. 'If you do not find an objective standing point from which to look back at yourself, you will always be egocentric, *identified* with yourself instead of in *relationship* to yourself.'[4]

We have begun to see (differently) now that we are not exclusively the self we mistake ourselves to be, the self we identify with. We can see, instead, that we are in relationship. There is an 'I', a witnessing presence, as Eckhart Tolle describes, who 'watches the thinker'. Consider that for just a moment: it *watches* the thinker. You have awakened; now watch! As you do, you will become more fully aware of the presence of this someone watching.

The important thing is to watch without judging (for judgment is part of the ego-driven response to the world around you). Notice, but do not judge. And as you do so, begin to accept the reality of who you are, warts and all. Remember, the egoistic self is the one that usually goes unobserved. This is not an exercise in trying to prove you are better than you are; quite the opposite, in fact. One of the dangers, as we attempt to become more fully whole through becoming more fully aware, is that we choose not to see the unhelpful things that reside in us – the addictions, for instance, or the anger, or the frustrations. If we feel as though we should be better than we are, or more popular, or successful, or funny, or clever… then our tendency is to sweep our shortcomings under the carpet, to pretend they are not there, and to look away because we don't like what we see.

Religious people can often end up putting on an act when they are with other religious people – becoming a certain type of person on a Sunday, for instance, at church, because they want to be accepted, or prove that they are 'holy' or 'spiritual', while being a quite different person for the rest of the week. Yet such dualism allows self-destructive traits to fester. If you truly notice your self in its entirety, what you see will begin to change, quite naturally. For, as Father Rohr writes, 'the truly self-destructive part… is exposed and falls away because it's now unnecessary. To see it is to defeat it, for evil relies on denial and disguise.'

Our task here is to begin to notice that you are in relationship with yourself. Instead of identifying with the image created for you by your ego-driven mind, spend time watching yourself, gently and without judgment. Pretence will begin to disappear as you see more clearly; you will come to know more of who you really are, and as you cease striving to prove or pretend or perform, whether to yourself or others (or even to God, who sees everything anyway!) then you will see with greater clarity your whole, real, made-in-the-image-of-God self. You will become more fully, deeply conscious.

Seeing others through fresh eyes

And in so doing, you will, of course, become more fully, deeply conscious of others. You will understand that they are ego-driven, too, but you will try less to judge them and use your weapons of attack and defence on them, and instead you will begin to see through their ego and into the person God created them to be.

Here's how John O'Donohue reflected on the mystery of togetherness and communion with others. 'Human presence is a creative and turbulent sacrament, a visible sign of invisible grace,' he wrote. 'Nowhere is there such intimate and frightening access to the mysterious. Friendship is the sweet grace that liberates us to approach, recognise and inhabit this adventure.'[5]

Our friendships and relationships can begin to help with our transformation; for this is the arena in which we see, and are seen; and in which we can be, even as we accept how others can be. We cannot and should not hope to change them; yet we can inspire those with whom we have relationship to see themselves more fully, by seeing them more fully ourselves. So often, we decide only to see the inadequacies, or the weaknesses, because we are trying to clamber over them in order to prove our own worth on the way to the 'top'. Yet, as we lay down the ego and rest more fully in who we were created to be, we help others to see that they are not 'the opposition' or 'the competition' but created beings who are in communion with us, and we with them.

How do you see those around you? It is time to see them through the eyes of grace, and wonder, and curiosity; with child-like expectation.

Seeing 'the world' around us with fresh eyes

You are already standing on holy ground. You don't need to be in a mosque or church or synagogue or temple to experience what is sacred. You don't need to make pilgrimage to a holy site (though that can be a transformative experience, most certainly). 'The earth is the Lord's,' says the psalmist, 'and everything in it.'[6] God is in you, God is in others, and the Spirit of God courses through Creation like a pulse, a heartbeat, a life-bringing, life-sustaining force for good.

One of the simplest ways to start seeing the earth differently is by noticing the way we have come to see it as something to be exploited and mined for our own gain. We tamed the wilderness and subdued the wildness and began to plunder the earth for our own material gain, at the cost of its true balance. As we begin to see ourselves differently, our view of our place within the world will also, necessarily, change. The world no longer revolves around us; it is not there simply as a resource, a commodity. Rather, as we understand ourselves more fully as people created by God and placed within the wider Creation, we can see that we are in relationship with the earth. And we can begin to see the earth in terms of what we can give to it, how we can care for it, and how we can love it as God's, not ours. If the earth were a person, we would all be guilty of abusing her; yet we *are* in relationship, and must begin to see what 'being in a relationship' means within this context.

* * *

Start to act

The next time you go for a walk, try actively to stop to 'watch the thinker' as you do so – in terms of the relationship between you and the scenery around you. Usually, you may simply appreciate the backdrop – the beautiful countryside or the amazing sky above – as a picture, something to be consumed. Try, instead, to stand back and see yourself within the picture as well. As you do, notice how you begin to see the world around you – and your place within it – very differently.

* * *

Seeing God with fresh eyes

God is within and without. Both of these ideas may surprise you. If you feel as though you are nothing but a worm, the idea that God is within you may catch you off guard. On the other hand, if you believe that this whole exercise of transformation is simply about your self, the idea that God exists outside of you, and can break into your life, may shock you.

Of course, ultimately God is a mystery that we cannot hope to solve. But we can still look for God, and attend to the *way* we look; because God is not a genie in a bottle, a cure-all for our ills, a winning lottery ticket in the game of life. God is God, and we find ourselves, ultimately, by finding God.

God is beyond us, literally and metaphorically. God is not something or someone that we use or control or whose purpose is to serve us (though God chose willingly to serve, as it happens). If we only look for God within, then we will not wholly find God. We must look outwards: to the sacred texts, to the prophets, to great works of art, to the sacredness of the mundane, to the faces of those around us who are made in God's image, and to the rest of God's Creation, of which we are a part.

Sometimes, we may see or hear or experience something that changes our view of God. I remember when the song 'One of us?' by Joan Osborne came out. 'What if God was one of us; just a stranger on a bus?' It helped me to see God in a slightly different light – to recognize that our view of God should be always deepening, broadening, because we will never see God in his or her entirety in this life. But as we saw with the story of Paul on the road to Damascus, sometimes God can surprise us by showing up, out of the blue, and we begin to see for ourselves... We should ask for, hope for, and expect to find God everywhere we look.

Yet God is within. Who, do you think, is the witnessing presence in your life, that presence who looks deeply into you and sees everything? Here, we discover an amazing paradox, a sacred, creative tension: as we gaze deeply, compassionately, beautifully upon our selves, and as we peel away the layers of our false self, we do so with the eyes of God, with the eyes of Spirit. As we contemplate, as we still ourselves, and as we reach out for God, we begin to find union with God within. The witnessing presence that has been there all along is the witness of God; we see with the eyes of God. And what we see is good.

* * *

Ultimately, our quest, then, is to look and see with the eyes of God; and as we do, the way we see ourselves, each other, the planet and God is transformed. For God sees everything – our fallibilities, our addictions, our ego-driven self that we must die to. And he also sees the infinite potential he has placed within us.

'Your eyes are windows into your body. If you open your eyes wide in wonder and belief, your body fills up with light,' said Jesus in Matthew 6:22. Seeing brings light, and with it, freedom.

As David Foster Wallace suggests, 'There are different kinds of freedom, and the kind that is most precious you will not hear much talked about in the great outside world of winning and achieving and displaying.

'The really important kind of freedom involves attention, and awareness, and discipline, and effort, and being able truly to care about other people and to sacrifice for them, over and over, in myriad petty little unsexy ways. That is real freedom.

'The alternative is unconsciousness, the default setting, the "rat race" – the constant gnawing sense of having had and lost some infinite thing.

'It is about simple awareness – awareness of what is so real and essential, so hidden in plain sight all around us, that we have to keep reminding ourselves, over and over: "This is water, this is water."'

Chapter 11

Living the change

All men dream: but not equally. Those who dream by night in the dusty recesses of their minds wake in the day to find that it was vanity: but the dreamers of the day are dangerous men, for they may act their dreams with open eyes, to make it possible.
T. E. Lawrence[1]

It is time to act; there is no point in gaining a deeper understanding of our place in life if it remains unrealized. But in readying ourselves for action, the great secret is to move *contemplatively* onwards, bearing the fruit of our reflection in the very heart of our action; bringing our true being most fully to bear on all of our doing.

This is a radical, repeating journey, from contemplation to action. As we move through this particular 'iconic journey', we now find ourselves ready to take the step into 'living from the true self' – but this is no one-off event. Instead, our task is to journey daily, along a narrow path that leads directly into the 'now', the present, and all that that means. This narrow path leads us towards becoming more fully present: present to ourselves, to each other, to the place we're in and to God.

This is, after all, no senseless journey, no aimless call to wander. As we go, we may look forward increasingly to *realizing* the call on our life – a call unique to us, to live our own life of incomparable, outwardly flowing beauty.

And here's the good news: we continue to discover who we are, not just by reflecting but also by engaging in action; *doing* things our own, unique way, proactively not reactively. The task, meanwhile, is to hold lightly to anything we specifically achieve, so that we leave less trace of ourselves, and more divine fingerprints of grace and love on all that we touch.

As we move from 'seeing the world afresh' into 'living it out', we must learn to reach out and touch the world precisely through our new way of being.

* * *

Stop to think
What mark have you secretly hoped to leave upon the world? What unique difference have you always wanted to make?

How much of that ambition has been driven by your ego? (Are you more concerned with nurturing your own sense of self and identity through your achievements, or with the fruit of those achievements themselves?)

How might your ambition change, as you awaken more fully to your whole self? How different might your plans and dreams look if you no longer feel the need to prove yourself or your worth to those around you, but can act simply and sincerely from a position of assurance?

How would you feel if you achieved great things yet left little trace of yourself through them? And how much more might you achieve if you focus on serving the higher cause in your life instead of making that higher cause *yourself*?

* * *

A confession

In Chapter 7 we touched on repentance – turning away from things that hinder, deliberately 'dying' to your ego-driven self so that you might come more fully alive to the person you were created to be. In the last chapter, we also thought about seeing ourselves with the eyes of God – in other words, seeing *everything*, acknowledging all that we are, and shining a light on everything in our life, especially the unobserved yet powerful ego-driven self.

Remember, 'evil relies on denial and disguise', as Father Richard Rohr says. It is easier to ignore or excuse the actions that are incompatible with the person you're trying to prove yourself to be; we end up wearing masks, pretending to be someone we're not, trying to fool ourselves and each other into believing our own hype.

Yet who, deep down, really wants to live a life of duplicity and pretence? I think we all know that a life of integrity – of centred, embodied 'wholeness' – will prove far more remarkable in the end than a life based on 'performance'.

This is why confession – a verbal acknowledgment of our repentance – can be a powerful part of the transformation process. If we confess our acts of duplicity or denial to ourselves, each other and God, we can bring them into the light and, by acknowledging them, let them go.

* * *

Start to act: confession 1

Start by confessing something to yourself, in a private, solemn moment of reflection. What's the one thing you do, perhaps in secret, which is least helpful to you or others? It is likely to be driven by the ego – though paradoxically it is likely, also, to be incompatible with the ego-driven image you may hope to project to a watching world. Name this part of your 'unobserved' self, without judgment. Speak it into the silence. Confess it out loud.

You might then, if you are brave, confess it to a good friend or confidante (or even a priest, if that is your tradition) – especially if your action has been affecting them. Ideally, this person will receive your confession without judging you (though it may be hard for them). Confessing something publicly will increase the likelihood that you can let it go, as you shine a light upon it.

Also, try confessing it to God. Ask for God's help to let it go. Stand back from your self, remembering that you are not your ego. See your broken, fragile, fallen self gently and compassionately through the witnessing presence within you; through the eyes of God. And resolve to try to walk more fully in the light from here on in, not because you have anything to prove to God or even yourself, but because it will lead you more fully into wholeness and peace within the present moment. For *now* is the time of your salvation.

* * *

Start to act: confession 2

Confession is not just about turning from the things that we dislike about ourselves and which we find hard to name or admit, however. It can also bring to light the things that we love that we might need to relinquish our attachment to as we begin living more fully from the true self.

Sometimes, we may need simply to hold more lightly to the things we love. If we have formed an unhelpful attachment to them – using them more to increase our self-esteem or serve our desires, for example – our hold can become suffocating. Sometimes, we have forgotten that we will even need to let go of the things we love in the end, when we face our ultimate journey through death into new life.

So, reflect upon the things that you love that you may need to 'surrender' or be *willing* to surrender. As you start living from your true self, relating to people and places not because of what you can take from them but because of how you can share yourself with them, your relationships may begin to feel different. Notice why.

There are different forms of love, of course. You may love chocolate – not for what you can do for it, but for what it can do for you. In a similar way, you may confuse your selfish desire for someone or something as 'love'; in relinquishing this, you will be freed actively to love them, even if that means freeing *them* from your grasp.

We thought above about the mark we hope to leave on the world, and asked whether we can leave smaller traces of ourselves and greater ones of the divine. You may wish to reflect, at this point, on how tightly you cling to the things you love, and as a consequence, what kind of marks your hands leave on those people or places or things.

Confess that you love these things, and try to imagine holding them more lightly – so that instead of clinging to them for fear of losing them, you are able to move forward in graceful coordination, like dancers.

* * *

Time out/Time in

In our overdriven culture one of the most difficult things to do is to take 'time out' to reflect on our being in the midst of our doing. If you have begun to do this, through contemplation and meditation, even through taking walks or going for a run and turning off the incessant chattering of your mind, you will have started to experience the practical benefits – becoming more fully present, calming down, gaining peace of mind, setting things in perspective, becoming more creative, discovering who you really are and what you really want to do.

The real test, however, is to bring the benefits of such 'time out' into your everyday work and life. It's what I call taking 'time in'. 'Time in' will help you to create a contemplative rhythm within the busyness of your schedule, and it will undoubtedly produce results. However, you have to have the strength and spirit of a warrior in order to make it happen. Remember, a warrior is someone who knows that something is worth fighting for – and fights for it. If peace of mind, increased creativity and presence are worth fighting for, then this is for you.

* * *

Stop to think
Draw up an honest schedule of your usual day-to-day activities. You will already have thought about this in Chapter 1 when we considered 'a life in the day' – a typical kind of day that is a reasonable representation of your life as 'a whole'. You may wish to revisit this list, or write another. Now, think about where you can factor in some 'time in' – such as short, sustainable periods of reflection and stillness that can embed the principles of contemplation within the maelstrom of your work or family life.

It may be that you drive to work, but always switch the radio on when you start the engine. Resolve to keep the radio turned off either on your way to work or on your way back – and use the time to still yourself.

It may be that before you switch your computer on, you can take 5 minutes to sit at your desk in silence, relaxing your shoulders and jaw, stilling your mind, and preparing proactively for a day of action through contemplation.

It may be, if you are a housewife or husband, that your child has a nap in the morning or at lunchtime; again, you could resolve to spend 5 minutes of that time in quietness, before you switch the TV on or go to sleep…

It may be that you always wear your mp3 player when you go the gym. Resolve not to play music for at least half the time you exercise, and use it, instead, to be 'still'.

Write yourself suggested moments for 'time in' on your schedule and try, as best as you can, to stick to them. You may wish to keep a journal that records your time in, and reflects upon the results for your work or your general sense of well-being. You may be surprised just what a practical difference it makes.

* * *

Start to act

Make sure you fight to turn these particular thoughts into action: the overpowering temptation is to always put the radio on, or check your emails straight away, or dive straight into work. If you go the usual route, you will keep acting from your false self, and the results will never be quite the same as if you have steadied yourself and entered the fray from the orientation of wholeness.

One of the main goals is to become more fully present – to your self, to your work, to your family (if you are at home), to your colleagues… The quality of your work will improve if you are focused on the work itself, rather than on the many things you have to get done beyond the task in hand. And the quality of your relationships will improve remarkably if you become fully present to the person who comes and asks for advice or for help when your mind is on other things.

So within your few minutes of quiet, shut the door (if you can), sit still, breathe deeply, and relax. Your work will wait for a few moments more. Overhear your chattering mind, which is straining to get on with everything; notice it, and let it go. You may wish to focus specifically on leaving the past where it is – acknowledging that you cannot rewrite recent mistakes, or trade forever on the glory of past successes. You could also focus on letting the future be. You do not live there; you live *here*. In fact, you can do nothing in the future; everything you achieve is firmly within the present.

So try to become more fully present by noticing your breathing, any sounds around you, any smells; notice small details in your room – colours, textures, shades... And simply inhabit the space that you have carved for yourself.

You will then be better prepared to face the onslaught of decisions and tasks to which you would usually react from your false or incomplete self. You may wish to end the mini-session with thoughts of gratitude for the people you work with, for the things you will be able to do today that will make a genuine difference, or simply for life itself. Gratitude will take you into the rest of your day from a place of rest, with a sense of openness and grace.

* * *

I once had a talk to prepare for an Easter event. It was a multimedia concert, with an orchestra, soloists, and images of Easter from the 'great masters', and the organizers had asked me to speak at it. This was a lovely request, and I had agreed; but as the day drew nearer, I was struggling to work out just what it was I needed to say. And I began to fear that my reputation as an interesting and evocative speaker might be dented if I failed to deliver.

As I sat at my desk getting nowhere fast, I decided to go for a run to clear my head. I thought, 'I can use the time to keep thinking about what I need to say.' But then I realized that the spiritually intelligent thing to do would be to quieten my mind instead, and seek inspiration from my whole self, and the Spirit within, not just my mind. So I dared to run without thinking about *anything* – noticing the times when my mind 'kicked in', but letting those thoughts slip away and subside.

As I became lost in the running, and more fully present to the countryside around me (seeing myself as part of the picture, instead of 'consuming' the scenery as though it were on TV), something arose within me – an idea for an angle that I would never have 'thought' of myself. It was the breakthrough I needed.

And in that moment, I was able to make a note of it, and continue contemplatively on my run without thinking any more about it. The period of quietening unlocked a creative idea for me that was better than anything I would normally have come up with. But it took a certain amount of guts, given the timescale, to use my time contemplatively instead of simply pressing on with the writing. Sometimes you have to hold the line and dare to do things differently.

You may have experienced something similar – an idea coming to you from 'left field', as they say. Think of when that happened, and what you were doing at the time. Often, it's when our mind is not focused on the task that we receive something from deep within, from that soulful space where our true self dances with the divine.

The tendency is, however, to keep busy, or (even worse!) to keep *looking* busy. It is very hard to go for a run during the day if you work at an office; it may be even harder to switch off your computer screen and sit there in silence, because it looks as though you are doing nothing. Which you are. But you're doing nothing for good reason.

Peace within the highs as well as the lows

As you seek actively to take 'time in' for yourself, try to remember that this place of stillness is one you should return to both within the trouble and turmoil *and* within the moments of joy and success. It's easy to see why a contemplative rhythm can work well for you when you're up against it; but you should try, if you can, to return to the place of stillness even when you have just registered a great achievement. In fact, it's important to do so.

The former England rugby union coach Sir Clive Woodward unusually used to keep his players back after a victory (instead of a defeat), to reflect on what went *right*. So often, we reflect on what went wrong, and how we can put things right. But it's crucial to consider why things go well. Added to that, it is your chance to ensure that you do not make unhealthy attachments to your success as it happens. 'Time in' will help you to hold lightly to the highs as well as the lows, and to be thankful for them without allowing them to swell your ego.

From understanding to realizing

There are different ways we can approach the art of taking spiritually intelligent action within our day-to-day lives, and we shall consider a few alternatives now. First, it's worth remembering that as we move from 'seeing' to 'living', we also move from understanding to *realizing*. No amount of knowledge or insight or understanding makes true sense unless it is realized – fleshed out in the actions of the story of your life.

'Understanding is the one-dimensional comprehension of the intellect,' writes Dan Millman in *The Way of the Peaceful Warrior*. 'It leads to knowledge. Realization is three-dimensional – a simultaneous comprehension of head, heart, and instinct. It comes only from direct experience.'[2]

At the most basic level, you begin to 'realize' you are entering a new way of being as you try things out. You must take small, manageable steps. But the journey of life is one of constant, deepening realization, and it culminates in the full realization of your full life's work.

* * *

Stop to think
Reflect on these words and what they mean for you:

I need to realize my potential.
I need to realize my potential rests in You.

* * *

Identifying the higher cause

Our actions are only truly meaningful when we understand the context in which we live and move and have our being. That's why we thought about the story we tell through our lives, in Chapter 8. Our own individual stories find their sense of purpose when we understand the Bigger Picture and the difference they can make to it.

Think in terms of what or whom you give yourself to – and what it is you're giving. Our lives are comprised of countless actions and transactions that contribute to our story: we give our time to our work or our colleagues or family; we give our energy to our hobbies; we give our talents in exchange for money or thanks... but all of these actions make up a greater whole, a whole that is sometimes easier to see when you look back on what you have been doing.

But we can't afford to wait until the end of our lives to discover whether or not we have acted with courage or passion or conviction. So it is worth projecting forward for a moment, in order to think how you might look back over 'the whole' of who you've become and what you've achieved.

'I wonder what stories will be told of us when we sit around the campfires of heaven?' I remember hearing those words, from the writer John Eldredge, and realizing that I'd been confronted with a powerful challenge. They're not meant as a threat; rather as an inspiration. But they focus the mind.

How would you like to be remembered? What, or who, will prove to be the overriding cause in your life, the cause to which (in retrospect) all of your smaller actions and transactions have contributed? To what or whom have you given your life? To what or whom have you given the gift of your self?

* * *

Stop to think
This may be the first time you have ever thought about your life in this way. It can be a sobering 'realization', and yet a liberating one, too.

You might like to think about who or what you are giving most of your time to right now.

Imagine you are 'sitting around the campfires of heaven'. What stories of your life will be talked about in excited tones around those fires? Who might be telling them?

To what or whom do you think you are giving your life?

To what or whom would you *like* to give your life?

How might that affect the time and energy you give to things within your typical day – such as TV, or general background noise, or defending or promoting yourself, or trying to accumulate possessions, or...

To what, or to whom, are you giving your heart?

* * *

Where have you buried your treasure?

There are certain things we treasure in life. The trouble is, they often diminish our hearts. We hold so tight to our treasure that our hearts get wrapped up, caught up, stashed away with the things we believe are most precious to us. Sometimes, we need to go in search of the treasure we have hidden away for so long to remind ourselves where it is we've left our hearts.

What is it that you treasure the most? And where have you stashed it? Sadly, most of us bury our treasure somewhere, for fearing of losing it. Is it buried away somewhere, where 'moth and rust can destroy it'? If it is, your heart is likely to be locked up there as well.

Some of us may need treasure maps just to show us where our hearts have been buried for all this time: beneath the house we stretched ourselves to the limit to buy; in the boot of the car that we bought on hire purchase; locked up in the kids' education; shackled in the boardroom; torn apart in the wrong bedroom…

* * *

Start to act
Reflect on where you have buried your treasure. Try drawing a map if it helps.

What does this say about where your heart may lie hidden?

What would you really love to treasure if you had the courage and the freedom to live as you would like to live, deep down?

How can your treasure map help you to think about living more dynamically from your heart? Try to draw an alternative map that shows the people or places or organizations with whom you could share your treasure.

* * *

Mapping the territory

Scott Peck writes, 'The world itself is constantly changing. Glaciers come, glaciers go. Cultures come, cultures go… Even more dramatically, the vantage point from which we view the world is constantly and quite rapidly changing…

'What happens when one has striven long and hard to develop a working view of the world, a seemingly useful, workable map, and then is confronted with new information suggesting that that view is wrong and the map needs to be largely redrawn?... What we do more often than not is to ignore the new information. Often this act of ignoring is much more than passive.'[3]

We have the choice: to oppose or ignore the new information, or to revise our maps. We can proceed through life lost, distracted, defeated; or we can turn each decision we must face into an opportunity to find our way through new terrain and redraw our map.

For it is how we choose to act, in the face of each dilemma or challenge that comes our way, that determines ultimately what becomes of us in the journey of life. This is no passive acceptance of our lot; instead, we travel towards wholeness and transformation through a proactive, decisive journey of the heart into the fullness that each moment offers us, and we offer each moment.

As the author Mike Riddell puts it, 'Neither past nor future provide legitimate respite from the challenge and beauty of the moment. When we learn to become fully present in every instant, we discover that there are opportunities and choices immediately before us which will determine both our past and our future.

'Here on the sharp blade of the moment lie opportunities to create and to love... In the capsule of experience which is given to us each instant, we determine who we are and what is significant to us. The whole of our lives is presented to us in the moment, and each moment is an intersection with eternity in which we decide our destiny and are offered the grace of becoming. All else is illusion.'[4]

Where are you willing to let the path lead you? To a place where few other paths seem to lead? To a place that has remained unmapped in your lifetime? To a place where you can find your treasure and share the joy with others? To a place of active surrender? To a place utterly incomparable with anywhere you could have imagined finding yourself?

The journey continues.

Chapter 12

Passing it on

*Life is a gift we receive each day. When we're closed, it's as though
we are asleep to the gift of life.*
Miriam Greenspan, psychotherapist[1]

Active service

As we near the end of our third journey through the icons, our
thoughts turn once more to 'passing it on'. It's crucial that we focus
firmly on how we serve others through the person we are becoming
(instead of telling other people how they should live) – passing on
the benefits of our own change, as we go, to those around us, and
in so doing, allowing deep once more to call to deep.

To make the most of who we are, what we 'do' should be in the
spirit of service. As we access our spiritual intelligence, we gain
a freedom to serve. Even if we do things for ourselves, they need
not be 'selfish' in the way we might have previously understood
it. Our actions gain greater significance when we understand how
they serve the higher cause in our life, and so even when we are
acting for ourselves, we have a choice about how and why we are
doing what we do.

It's perhaps worth remembering David Foster Wallace's words
from Chapter 10 before we proceed: 'The really important kind
of freedom involves attention, and awareness, and discipline,
and effort, and being able truly to care about other people and to
sacrifice for them, over and over, in myriad petty little unsexy ways.
That is real freedom.'

First steps towards the life of service

The greatest act of service, both to yourself and to those around you, is to start by surrendering any temptation or compulsion to live up to what others expect of you – and what you expect from your self. All such expectation is false (despite the fact that you may have used some people's expectations of you as a spur).

We must lay down such expectations, for they provoke the incessant chattering of the mind, which feeds voraciously on them and creates an imaginary person out of them on our behalf. Instead, on the narrow path towards wholeness, we must come to know who we really are, which values we choose to live by, and what lies at the very centre of our being – that soulful interface between our true self and the divine. It's only then that we can begin to live according to who we were created to be, not according to what other people expect or demand us to become.

Steve Jobs, the founder of Apple, once gave a stirring speech (that you can now see online) to Stanford graduates. He spoke candidly about the fact that we are a long time dead, and of the importance of living in the light of this truth. 'Your time is limited,' he said, 'so don't waste it living someone else's life. Don't be trapped by dogma, which is living with the results of other people's thinking. Don't let the noise of other people's opinions drown out your own inner voice. And most important, have the courage to follow your heart and intuition; they somehow already know what you truly want to become. Everything else is secondary.'[2]

We will never fully live up to expectations; none of us does. We all fall short of each other's hopes for, or demands upon, us. And we fall short of our own hopes and demands constantly.

But the spiritually intelligent life is not about trying to please people, or impress them (or ourselves). It's not about getting people to like us, even though we should be sensitive to their needs and seek to serve others in all that we do. Instead, we should try to live increasingly from the assurance of who we really are, with integrity, choosing what is right within each moment in service of our higher cause – the greater good to which we give ourselves most fully.

In such a way, we will no longer be *reactive* to the hopes and expectations of others; however, paradoxically, we will find ourselves serving them more effectively as a result.

Today's world pulls and pushes us in myriad directions; it impels us to present different personas within different situations and to 'perform', whether in the boardroom or the bedroom. We act out our various roles, but in doing so, we become social chameleons, fitting in, not standing out and standing up for something greater. The way to steer a meaningful path throughout our relationships and 'life worlds' (as sociologists call them) is to live with increasing integrity, becoming true to our self, to each other and to God, within each situation in which we find ourselves.

And so, we begin to taste the greatest freedom when, instead of serving our self or our vain ambition, we choose willingly to lay down our fear-driven sense of identity-through-doing and open our eyes to the possibility of selfless service through self-giving love.

Of course, we need to know ourselves before we can die to ourselves; and we must go through the journey of 'growing up' precisely in order to understand the boundaries our ego has tried to create for us, so that we may transcend them and enter life more fully.

It is in the laying down that we begin to live. And as we recognize and actively lay down our desires, temptations, yearnings and cravings, we will experience a radical taste of freedom. We find that we are no longer slaves to our self or others; instead, we may begin to live our own, unique life, infused with the unique talents and strengths we have been given. Instead of this being a life to live up to, we might instead see it as a dance... a dance with the divine source of life.

* * *

Stop to think

Try to take a step back from the question, 'What stories will be told about us when we sit around the campfires of heaven?' to ask, more immediately, 'Whose life am I living right now?'

You can only begin to live truly *for* others if you lay down their expectations (and your egoic ones) and begin to live your own life first.

You might like to write a list of the people in your life whose expectations continue to shape your actions unhelpfully. Why not talk to the people you identify about this?

Now, write a list of the people in your life *you* expect things from. How can you begin to release them from your own unhelpful expectations, so that in turn you may help them to live more fully as the person they were created to be? How can you begin to pass on the benefits of your own transformation in this way?

* * *

Demonstrating leadership

As you begin to release your self from unhelpful expectations, and to identify your higher cause, you will start to demonstrate to others how your story can make sense within – and make sense of – the Bigger Picture. You will be able to tell that story through how you live that story.

No longer will you receive passively what is placed in front of you in life, for example; no longer will you simply take what you can from the Bigger Picture. No longer will you feel powerless in the face of unfolding events, or crushed by the weight of the world. Instead, you will give your *self* to the Bigger Picture, and offer what only you can truly offer – according to the values of your heart.

You will find yourself on active service, a spiritual warrior, showing that there is a cause worth fighting for – a cause so disarming that you are willing to surrender all to its service.

And so, you will become a natural leader to those around you – not by telling them what to do, or by shouting the loudest, but by showing them a different way. Not that they must walk your path, necessarily; they must find their own. But they must get up off the sofa and start walking!

The serenity of true service

So, one benefit of your transformation is being able to show other people the way. Another is that your relationships will be transformed. You will no longer try to kid others that you have more – or less – to offer than you do. When we act in true service, we can act in increasing confidence, because we have nothing to lose. There is no pretence that we are someone we're not; instead, we are giving what we can of who we are; no more, no less.

This is true whether you are simply attracted to someone romantically or trying to win a contract or running for the presidency of the United States! You are freed to do what you have been placed on earth to do best: be yourself.

Such confidence is infectious and attractive. Remember, you are at your best when you remind yourself that you are utterly incomparable. The moment you sense that someone else might be better at a task, or someone else is more talented or gifted at such and such, you enter defensive mode, trying only to consolidate your position. When you stop comparing yourself to others, you enter the freedom that comes with knowing that no one but you can possibly do what you do best, especially when it is offered in the spirit of serving others, not one's self. You will never enter a business meeting in the same way again!

What does it profit a man if he gains the world but loses his soul?

The words of Jesus provide a useful reminder here. What does it profit a person if they gain the world but lose their soul?[3] In our consumer culture, it's easy to see how we can all race after quick profit by selling ourselves short; putting on hold our ethics, our instincts, our natural sense of what's right or wrong, in order to get what we want from life. But such behaviour always leaves us feeling bereft – no amount of material comfort (beyond the most basic needs for survival) will ever match the sense of following your true calling, living from your heart.

The soulful, narrow path of surrender may seem like it's all about loss; in fact, it's about the greatest kind of profit imaginable. For you will profit by regaining your soulfulness. And this is the best position from which to help others profit from your transformation – because you will find that what you have to give increases immeasurably. Instead of hoarding treasure for yourself, you will be looking actively to share the treasures of your heart.

Living your brand

We are painfully 'brand-aware' within Western culture: most of us have favourite brands; many of us construct a sense of identity for ourselves through the very brands we buy and the logos that we wear. This can be profoundly unhelpful, of course, as so many people seek identity through a logo alone. Yet we can use our sense of brand-awareness positively to think more closely about the deeper brand we choose to live by, and about the brand values we demonstrate through love to those around us. (Remember: we are not all clones; we are uniquely created, with unique combinations of the way we see and touch the world.)

* * *

Stop to think
What are your favourite consumer brands? What do you hope they'll say about you when you buy them or wear them or parade them? What are the 'brand values' you're attracted to? How do they seem to build a sense of identity for you, however superficially?

* * *

Beyond skin deep

Advertisers talk of us being 'loyal' to particular brands. We probably *are* all loyal to certain brands, whether we aware of it or not, and whether we like it or not. It's not always a conscious decision, but something about the brand appeals to us and encourages us to demonstrate our loyalty. Sometimes we buy an item of clothing because of the logo itself, and what we think it says about us.

Today, some people have become so 'loyal' to their logos that they have even had them tattooed on themselves. It's hard to believe, but it's true. The most popular logos to be tattooed onto human skin include the Nike Swoosh and the Apple logo. Both brands have inspired such fierce loyalty from their customers that people suffer pain to bear a mark that will remain burned onto their skin for the rest of their life.

Our logos demonstrate our sense of belonging; a brand was originally, of course, a mark burned onto an animal (or slave) to denote ownership. Have you ever thought that the brands you wear or display say something about whom you belong to?

Most people of course don't get a tattoo of a corporate logo; but many people do have tattoos. It's a cultural phenomenon in the West, in fact. Whatever you think about tattoos, they are a way of demonstrating to other people something profound about your self and your sense of identity and allegiance: the names of the people you love, perhaps, or spiritual symbolism which is pertinent to you, or the football crest of the team you'll support until you die...

* * *

Stop to think
If you were to get a tattoo, what would you have done? Think very seriously about this (even if you would never have a tattoo in your life!), because a tattoo can be a deeply personal representation of who you really believe yourself to be. You have to think very carefully, because it will be very painful to have done, and it will never be removed. So what permanent sign of belonging or relationship or allegiance would best sum you up? Perhaps it would be a symbol, a name, a phrase or a picture. You might draw it in your journal, just to remind you.

What would that mark say about you – about who you are, what or whom you love, to whom you belong, or what is most important to you?

* * *

Start to act
You don't need a tattoo, of course, to live by a set of values that you hold dear and to be able to express or articulate those values. But as you begin to live more freely from your true self, then now is a good time to remind yourself of those values, and to ask yourself how you might wish to clarify and express them as you go forward.

Many companies today have a list of 'corporate values'. If you had a statement of 'Brand You values', what would they be? If any seem more to do with your ego than your true self, what do you wish to do with them?

Perhaps there is a statement – instead of a list – that would best sum up the way you wish to live, and the values you wish to adhere to within any situation you find yourself in. 'Living your brand' is a helpful way of thinking about how you proceed with integrity through every situation you find yourself in.

The prophet Micah spoke of 'acting justly, loving mercy and walking humbly'.[4] It's a short set of words that could potentially determine how you live your entire life. The Torah (which Christians count as the first five books of the Old Testament) suggests that the Law can be summed up in the words, 'Love God, love your neighbour'. Again, this is a very succinct phrase through which an entire life can be expressed and a whole life lived.

What set of words – either your own, or something you have read or seen – would best describe your 'brand values'? Try to write or find something that would come closest.

* * *

As you reflect upon a set of values to live by, it's important to be able to remember them and express them, so that you are always 'bringing them to life' – realizing them, if you like. For values are nothing unless they are brought off the page and into life.

Many people have never been challenged or encouraged to think about the values they live by; it is a product of our spiritually dumb culture that we do not equip ourselves to live with integrity in such a way. Yet this is a gift you can bring to others, by expressing your values clearly and succinctly through how you live. Your short phrase, or your imaginary tattoo, may help you to help others begin to think about their own values. You can help to 'pass it on' as soon as you begin to realize some of the potential for living from the values at your heart.

Just as a tattoo is a talking point, and just as a branded T-shirt actively communicates something about what you love or who you are, so too your own sense of 'Brand You' can demonstrate to others a commitment to a higher cause, a life of service, a unique way of seeing or touching the world.

And it can help you, at every twist and turn of the plot of your life, to live passionately and unswervingly from your heart. You might think of it as your moral compass. Act with soul.

* * *

Trusting your conscience

Another way to think about this is by considering your 'conscience'. Ask yourself what your 'conscience' really is and where it comes from. You might think of it as a still, small voice somewhere deep within, a voice that tries to keep you on track, to help you do the right thing.

As you become more fully conscious or awake, you will find that you begin to access your 'conscience' more fully. You will become more closely attuned to it, noticing it more clearly as you quieten the louder voice of your ego.

You might think of it as your sense of soulfulness, or indeed as your soul itself – the interface at the deepest point of your self, between the divine and the fully human. As you overhear your true self more closely, you will learn to hear and follow your 'conscience' more powerfully.

* * *

Stop to think
When was the last time you heard the voice of your conscience? What did it ask you to do? Did you act upon it?

You might like to keep a note in your journal of the times, moving forward from here, when you think you hear the voice of your conscience, and an account of what it is telling you.

Where does your 'conscience' come from, do you think? How can it help you to act with integrity? What is the relationship between your conscience and your 'Brand You'?

* * *

Love your enemies

Active service takes you further into the mystery of life than you might ordinarily be prepared to go. The path may lead into places that are hostile or that demand sacrifice. This is no soft option. Instead, you are on a journey of self-mastery, discipline and commitment to the narrow path. You need a dogged determination simply to become fully present.

But you need great courage to confront and disarm your enemies by seeking the benefits of your transformation for them, too. The good news is that you can help to break the cycle of violence in this world that is perpetuated through the ego by doing a simple yet miraculous thing: loving your enemies.

You love them first by dissolving the category between friend and enemy. All people are people. Enmities are created by the ego, within the context of our painful fall from grace. We react in fear to each other, instead of love, as our ego seeks to create a distinct identity of 'you' *as opposed to* anyone else. But as you lay down your ego, the opposition can disappear.

Then it's a matter of seeing all comers through your new, spiritual eyes – not as potential enemies but in a far deeper, richer way.

Mike Riddell writes: 'One of the keys to spiritual growth is to look on each new person we encounter along the way as someone who has been sent to us with a gift. They have some lesson to teach us, some quality to awaken in us, some blessing to bestow on us, some need for us to fulfil, or some question to ask of us.'

He continues, 'When we regard people in this way, we cease to look on even the apparently most obnoxious as enemies, and rather begin to probe for their essential mystery. It is astonishing how such a simple change of orientation toward people can release grace and discovery for those willing to try it. But first we must learn to overcome our prejudice and fear.'[5]

The question is, are you willing to 'overcome your prejudice and fear'? Of course, if you change the way you see your enemies, you will not only benefit them, you will also benefit yourself – releasing yourself from the demands of your ego and actively beginning to practise the art of letting your inner depths speak to the depths of others. You may just find yourself – as well as many others – liberated from years of bondage to past hurts and wounds, and future fears and insecurities.

* * *

Stop to think: what is your gift?
If you're to see the gifts in other people, you ought first to reflect on the gifts you have yourself. We are not always very good at thinking positively about ourselves (in a non-egoic way), but it is vital that we do. Think of a gift you have that is somehow special to

you. What have people noticed about you that seems to be 'given', somehow, to you – something you do beautifully, without too much effort?

Now, think about how you 'give' your own gift to others. How do they benefit? What joy do they derive from your gift? How do you use it, on occasions, for the benefit of others?

How would you like to use your gift in the active service of others – and not just friends, but your enemies, too?

* * *

As we come to the end of this third journey through the icons, let's finish by remembering that while it may be better to give than to receive, we ought to practise our receiving as well. For other people have gifts of their own, which will strengthen, challenge and inspire us. We can only receive them, however, if we open ourselves to those around us, and approach them not defensively, but in the spirit of communion.

So often in our culture, we feel as though we need to earn the right to receive anything; we must work to earn money, and if we lose our job and have to receive benefits, we feel the stigma of getting something for nothing. And so, in receiving from others, we may feel undeserving, or we may feel that we have to reciprocate the 'gift' – which is hard if that gift is, for example, lavish hospitality. There is, of course, an important distinction to be made between receiving and taking; but still, many of us find it hard to receive in the right spirit.

Ultimately, it is only through receiving from the Spirit of God that we can practise receiving with no fear of strings attached. For the gift of life flows to us, through Spirit; yet we have done nothing to deserve it. We simply *have* to receive it. And we don't just receive *from* the Spirit. We receive the Spirit itself, which flows through us and sustains life. If we refuse to receive the Spirit, we will most likely refuse to receive most other things in life; just as, if we refuse to receive other people, we will never be able to receive *from* them.

This is what communion is. It is the radical interdependence of life; of giving and receiving, trusting and opening our hearts to others and, by accepting their gifts, affirming and celebrating them.

We need humility to receive from others, and self-assurance; by receiving, you are helping others to give themselves, and you are meeting them by opening yourself up too.

'How can we give to life if we haven't learned to receive from life?' asks Mary Saunders, a practitioner in Chinese medicine for more than twenty years. She has a point. 'Life is a gift we receive each day. When we're closed, it's as though we are asleep to the gift of life,' says Miriam Greenspan, a psychotherapist. Both are quoted in a wonderful article called 'Open Hands, Open Heart' in *Ode Magazine*.[6] As we enter the final leg of this particular journey, we will gain most, and give most, if we do so with an open, receptive spirit, in active service.

Level 4

Living in 'flow'

Chapter 13

Awakening

The world's a puzzle; no need to make sense out of it.
Dan Millman[1]

Buckle your seatbelt, Dorothy, 'cos Kansas City is going bye bye.
Cypher to Neo, in *The Matrix*

Toto, I don't think we're in Kansas City any more.
Dorothy, in *The Wizard of Oz*

In this final journey through the icons, we turn our attention to 'flow' – the creative, dynamic flow between our being and our doing. At this level, we must try to inhabit mystery, understanding that we do not need to know all of the answers in order to become spiritually mature.

Whose reality?

Life is not a film, and we're unlikely to be transported by tornado to Oz, like Dorothy and Toto, or awakened from the death-sleep of the Matrix by taking the red pill, like Neo.

But these myths do, of course, help us to explore 'reality' more powerfully. (The writer Marcus Borg, citing German novelist Thomas Mann, suggests that a myth is 'a story about the way things never were, but always are'.[2]) We should, if we stay committed, awake one day to realize that, as those films suggest, life is not all that it seems. There is far more going on than meets the eye.

If you've seen the film *The Truman Show*, you'll remember that Truman was born into a reality TV film set, and knew no differently until, in his adult life, he started noticing cracks in the façade of the world in which he was living, and began to awaken to the fact that there was a world beyond the confines of the life he imagined to be true. It is a powerful metaphor for our own small lives, which many of us live in an unthinking daze, oblivious to any greater possibilities. Truman was never living his own life – his choices were contrived by Christof, the reality show's director, and by the viewers of the show. Remember what Steve Jobs said: *'Your time is limited, so don't waste it living someone else's life.'*

Why didn't Truman awaken earlier to the unreality of his life? Because, as Christof tells one of his workers, 'we accept the reality of the world as it is presented to us'. We must stop accepting that version of reality if we are to unleash the potential of our spiritual intelligence. But it takes courage and strength to do so.

A word of warning, however. As we begin this final leg of our four-part journey, we must accept that no frame or model like the one in this book will ever lead us into complete awakening. It is simply a way of trying to gather fragments of truth and evoke new possibilities. This is not gospel, and it is crucial to surrender our attachment to any models such as this as we go. The journey from here is yours to make. This is your chance to awaken to your own possibilities of an alternative reality, even on *this* side of the rainbow.

And it will be up to you to become open, watchful; ready to take notice and to take responsibility for your awakenings. They can and will arrive, as we have already noticed, in different forms. But as they accumulate, you may one day realize that the world, for you, has changed, and the nature of its reality has altered forever.

In the book of Genesis, the patriarch Jacob famously dreamed of a ladder 'resting on the earth, with its top reaching to heaven, and the angels of God ... ascending and descending on it.'[3] As John Eldredge suggests, 'He wakes, more awake than he's ever been in his life, thanks to the dream, and realizes for the first time that there is more going on around him than he ever imagined. "Surely the Lord is in this place, and I was not aware of it," he reflects.'[4] God is in and around you, if only you were to realize the truth of that. You are standing on holy ground, for all ground is holy in God's world, in reality.

Awakening to the treasure we've been carrying all along

Some time ago, I experienced an awakening that has stayed with me powerfully. I was visiting a retreat centre for a day's reflection on my own, and I couldn't sit still for long without wanting to find something to 'do'. So I went for a walk. Thankfully, it was a walk through lovely countryside, and I was able to still my restless mind and begin to find a place of calm beyond the chattering of my ego.

As I walked a footpath alongside a ploughed field, my hands were cold and so I put them in my pockets. I felt a little stone there amid the loose change and keys that must have been there for several days. I remembered that my son had given it to me: 'This is treasure,' I could recall him saying, 'and I want *you* to have it.' Straight away, I remembered the words of Jesus, too: 'For where your treasure is, there your heart will be also.'[5]

I reflected, as I walked, on how I can bury myself in the many false things I treasure (as we considered in Chapter 11), and I considered gratefully – attentively – the treasure I had just rediscovered. It was then that it dawned on me why it's worth making space for your self. All you need is a little gap to open within your everyday busyness, and you might find something you'd neglected, which you've been carrying all along. I keep that little stone with me to remind me of this awakening.

It's often in the smallest details that we discover the biggest revelation. If we are looking too hard for the grand vision or the writing in the sky, we may miss what has been placed within the ordinariness of life – and within our hearts – for us to discover from the start. Sometimes it's a question, as I say, of awakening to what has already been given to us.

Awakening to the magic

There comes a wonderful point on the journey towards wholeness when we must learn to expect the unexpected. That's the place in which we can truly awaken to where we are and to how things can be. Think of it in terms of magic. We talk about the 'magic of Christmas' and allow ourselves to enter a world in which, for a short time at least, we can be open to the possibilities of angels in the sky singing 'peace on earth'; and to God becoming one of us, 'Emmanuel' – meaning 'God with us', born into poverty, surrendering everything, and turning the world upside down in the process.

Sometimes, you need to place yourself deliberately in the position of expectancy (as natural leaders seem to do). Believe that great things can happen, and commit to your path. If you give providence a little room to act, exciting things begin to emerge. Speaking of the way some people seem to 'make things happen', the spirituality and business guru Peter Senge writes, 'It would be wrong to say that highly successful innovators expect magic to occur, but they somehow accept it quietly, as an almost inevitable part of the process.'[6] He suggests that sometimes it's about being deliberately open to what *wants* to happen. Not just what might happen – but what *wants* to happen.

* * *

Stop to think

Can you remember a time when something magical, unexpected, coincidental or providential happened to you? What do you think 'wanted' to happen? Did you let it?

How did this little bit of magic in your life affect you? Did you receive it as a gift? Did it disturb you?

How could you begin more proactively to expect the unexpected? Do you need to surrender a little more control of your life, to allow for the unexpected to work its own magic? If so, how can you make room? What things do you still need to lighten your grip on?

* * *

A return to fresh experience

As we make room for the unexpected, we must simultaneously awaken to our greater union with the world around us – to the people we're with and the place we're in and the Spirit that breathes through it all. We awaken to what *wants* to happen through us as we open ourselves to the possibility of giving our self to a higher cause and making our providential – non ego-driven – mark. Your life may take an unexpected twist as you surrender the plans your own mind has fearfully created for you. You may choose the path of love instead.

When did you last feel wonderfully surprised by life? Contemplation can help, if you can't remember when that was. It helps us to experience the world afresh, as we surrender our usual responses and become present to something more positively unpredictible. Instead of straining into the future to try to make your plans come true, you may respond in wonder within each changing moment. As you open your self to the possibilities of a little magic in your life, you can put to death the restrictive expectations and demands of your false self, and start to receive the unimaginable.

We can all awaken to spontaneity. And in so doing, we can break the vicious circle of ego that has bound us, entering one of virtue instead – a virtuous circle of creativity, freedom, awe and celebration. Those who have already broken the cycle are – as we all know – wonderful people to have around. They will not settle for banality, nor become a victim of their own selfish thought patterns. They live open, generous, inspiring and unexpected lives.

This is a vivid new place to find your self within, most certainly. A new, previously unimagined kind of reality, yet one that was prepared for you from the beginning of time.

Stranger in a strange land

Where do you feel most at home? The apostle Paul talked of being a 'citizen of heaven', living on earth. A resident alien, if you like. Think back to when you travelled in a foreign country. It can be frightening, challenging, inspiring; your senses are heightened, you feel wide *awake* somehow. You may feel different, exposed even. You may notice the tiniest things about yourself as well as others. And even though it can be hard and sometimes intimidating to be a stranger in a strange land, it can also make you feel 'alive'.

Paul was not saying that we should spend our days dreaming of escape from earth to where we truly belong, heaven; but imploring us to find our identity in something or Someone not entirely of this world, and to act from a very different set of values and expectations to the ones we usually experience on our travels through the place we no longer call home. In so doing, we may awaken to the possibility of finding hope within hopelessness, creating shards of light within darkness, bearing first-fruits of a new world to taste right here, right now.

Jesus said, mysteriously, that 'the kingdom of God is at hand'.[7] It is all around us, if we did but realize it. Such a kingdom is not of this world, yet it will find its place in our being and doing – in the hearts and lives of those in this world who awaken to it, and who are open to the possibility of fulfilling their God-given potential.

Jesus used many different images to describe the nature of its reality – the kingdom, he taught, is like a man who finds treasure in a field, and sells all he has to buy the plot. It is like a seed, which grows into a great tree in which the birds can find shelter and rest. It is like a 'pearl of great price'.[8]

What image might you use for an alternative, in-breaking world?

Just another lifestyle choice?

It is one thing to glimpse possibilities; it is another to enter fully into those possibilities. You cannot buy your way in, of course; you can't lift a new way of being and doing from the shelf and indulge yourself for a while in the trappings of what may seem like a cool, counter-cultural lifestyle choice.

Contemplation is not a trendy new tool, a badge to wear or a mere talking point at a dinner party. If it becomes something to boast about, we've turned it into an ego-driven practice. That's why our focus should not fall upon ourselves ultimately, but on God. For this is no self-centred journey, after all. It is not about a feel-good course that delivers a feel-good factor for life. God is not a commodity to be bought or sold, to enhance your personal sense of spiritual mystique.

Ultimately, we must not even attach ourselves to the experiences – magical, contemplative, or other-worldly – that may awaken us to a whole, new way of being. Instead of feeding on the experiences alone, we will need to use them to find the entrance to the kingdom itself, and walk right through into a permanent state of wakefulness.

Entering fully

For the Pevensie children who entered the world of Narnia, the passage was in the form of a wardrobe. It was a gateway to a world of magical possibilities, an entirely other way of seeing, understanding and living in another kingdom. They walked through the wardrobe and into a world of wonder.

Now, you may get a bump on the head if you try to walk through your own wardrobe. I'm sure many children have tried it. It's not something that really happened, but the myth speaks of truth, of the way things *are*.

Jesus used the image of a gate in the city wall at Jerusalem called 'the eye of the needle'. 'It is easier,' he told his followers, 'for a camel to get through the eye of a needle than for a rich man to enter the kingdom of heaven.'[9] We all have an awful lot of baggage – whether material or emotional or spiritual – to lay down before we can enter through what is clearly a narrow gate, a small opening into a different world. It is both hard to find and hard to enter with all the stuff we carry.

The path to life that leads through such an opening, Jesus reflects, is narrow, 'and few find it'. This seems like an odd thing to say for a spiritual leader. Wouldn't you want to 'sell' your spiritual programme, open it up for everyone, increase the number of your followers, claim credit for starting a movement? Well, you would if you were seeking to become a spiritual leader through your own ego-driven motives. But a true leader will lead people into truth; and the truth is that very few people in this world manage to pass through the gate, or find the path beyond, let alone walk it.

The birth passage

A man called Nicodemus once approached Jesus in the dead of night, asking what he must do to enter life. Now, Nicodemus was no slouch. He knew the ancient scriptures in his head; he was a teacher of the Law. And yet he had not found the gate or the path that leads to life. He was trapped – but crucially, he recognized it.

'You must be born again,' said Jesus.[10] It's another metaphor involving a narrow passage that brings you into a whole, new world. If you are truly to die to your self and your ego, and to enter the new world, the magic kingdom; if you are to find the path that leads to life and not just glimpse it from afar but begin to walk it, then you must be born again. Think of the caterpillar and the butterfly. You reach a point of no return. You turn, and turn into the child of God you were created to become. You become a new creation. The old has gone; the new has come.

Imagine: it's the kind of thing that can only happen when you begin to expect the unexpected.

Chapter 14

Seeing afresh

I pray that the eyes of your heart may be enlightened.
Ephesians 1:18

Mystics are the eyes of the Body... They maintain that awestruck outlook towards the infinite. In them, the life of prayer informs the life of action; their contemplation of Reality makes all that they do more real.
Evelyn Underhill[1]

The link between wakefulness and watchfulness

We have reflected upon what it could mean to move into a state of more permanent wakefulness, using our many small 'awakenings' to help us to become fully awake. Now, as we proceed to the next icon, 'seeing afresh', for the last time on this journey, let's consider the relationship between wakefulness and watchfulness.

A gate. A wardrobe. The eye of a needle. A birth canal. At the entrance to the whole, new world of which we are invited to become a citizen, we arrive at a point of no return. As we do, if we are willing, things need never be the same again: we won't just glimpse the world differently, but will begin to see, to observe, to watch, and to become more fully conscious – in the course of everyday life – of life itself.

Peter Senge sees this transformation as U-shaped – surrender on the path of descent down the U, transformation at the bottom, and then action in the path of ascent on the other side. 'At the bottom of the U,' he writes, 'lies a sort of inner gate, which requires us to drop the baggage we've acquired on our journey.' He writes of the mystery of 'letting go and letting come'. As we move through the U, he says, we 'begin to see from within the source of what is emerging, letting it come into being through us'. Here is the mystery: we will never see what is emerging through us until we let go of what we *think* should be emerging through us. The goal is not to force anything to emerge, but to watch it come as we let go.

At the start of this U is the world 'as it is' – the world we need to observe and become fully aware of. On the right-hand side of the U is the world 'coming into being through us'. As we emerge through the bottom of the U (through retreating and reflecting), the world starts to come into being through us. It's a helpful way of understanding it. Here, 'the self turns into a source through which the future can begin to emerge'.

Some of the people Senge has interviewed who have experienced times of profound personal transformation describe the bottom of the U as a 'membrane' or a 'threshold'. 'Some even saw it as a type of death-and-rebirth cycle,' he writes. 'Letting go and surrendering belong to the death part of this cycle, while the coming into presence of a different sense of self seems to belong to the early stages of a new birth.' [2]

The narrowest gap of the present

However we wish to see it, the narrowest gap (the bottom of the U, or the gate or threshold or membrane) is only to be found within the present – and, mysteriously enough, can be understood as the present itself. 'Find the "narrow gate that leads to life,"' says Eckhart Tolle. 'It is called the Now. Narrow your life down to this moment...' [3]

This is truly a radical, spiritually intelligent way of seeing. Transformation will never happen in the past or the future, because past and future are simply illusion – our way of understanding what has happened, or what we think will happen. But nothing now happens there. They are comprised of memories and yearnings, attachments that our ego has made for us. Unless we let these go, we will be caught for the rest of our days living in the past or yearning for the future – illusions that simply don't exist.

The narrow gap we really need to pass within is right here, in the present. And the opportunity to be transformed within this narrowest of spaces is present with us every day. It's just that we can't usually see it for looking.

Even if we understand that we need to look for a gate or pass through a membrane or the eye of the needle, we remain in danger of believing that it's something we will one day discover, somewhere further down the track. This is not true. Though it's hard to find, it is only available within the present.

Tolle reminds us how to become more fully present through *the way we watch*. 'Use your senses fully. Be where you are. Look around. Just look, don't interpret. See the lights, shapes, colours, textures. Be aware of the silent presence of each thing. Be aware of the space that allows everything to be… Allows the 'isness' of all things. Move deeply into the Now.'[4]

It sounds simplistic, but the art of becoming more fully present – to everything around you, to yourself, to your tasks, to your family, to God – is intrinsically caught up with observing the world around you without judgment, moving from seeing the world as a set of images to be consumed to understanding that you are part of the picture, within this present moment. It may help, simply, to look at your hand, or your leg, and observe it within the context of the room you are in. See that you are neither subject nor object but divinely related to everything around you.

Dan Millman notes that his own journey of discovery – involving discipline, sacrifice, discovery, self-mastery, death and life – lasted for years before he began to realize that he was looking for a gate. His spiritual mentor, whom he called Socrates, told him, 'Your business is not "to get somewhere" – it is to be here. Now is the time to apply yourself like never before, if you're to have even a chance of finding the gate. It is here before you; open your eyes, now!'[5]

The reason we struggle to find the gate is because we search for it in the realm of illusions instead of looking for it precisely where we are. It is here, not somewhere else.

* * *

Stop to think

Are you *still* trying to get somewhere? If so, where is it?

How does your desire to get to that place distract you from being here, now?

Do you become so fixed on completing a task that you never stop to savour the process itself? Are you so worried about getting through the week that you never enjoy the days? Do you drive so fast to reach your destination that you don't savour the process of getting there, with all the opportunities for quietness or communion that a journey affords?

The gate is in the present; yet all the while you are straining forward to 'arrive', you never will.

* * *

Rediscovering awe

Evelyn Underhill, a twentieth-century author and Christian mystic, wrote about the way mystics – those people who have 'conscious communion with God, and always a communion of love' – don't just see with the eyes; they become eyes. 'Mystics are the eyes of the Body,' she wrote. 'They maintain that awestruck outlook towards the infinite.'[6]

Thank goodness for those people who have gone before us, who have seen mysteries we may never ourselves have seen, but who, through their seeing, help us to see. As we begin to live within the present, we too can begin to see the world around us afresh in each moment, and become eyes for those around us.

It is quite something to see the infinite. Yet the mystics do not look far off into the distance to see it; they do not need some kind of supernatural telescope. For the infinite is not measurable in never-ending space and time, but is beyond time. It simply *is*. Here and now. The infinite transcends time, does away with it. Eternal life starts here.

Of course, we need time and space to know certain things – where and when to go to work or how long to boil an egg, and so on. But as we begin to see with awestruck eyes beyond the confines of past and future, time melts into the infinity of the continuous present.

This does not, however, mean that we simply float around in some kind of spiritual daze. The beauty of accessing and unleashing our spiritual intelligence flows from our being into our doing. Underhill says of the mystics that 'in them, the life of prayer informs the life of action; their contemplation of Reality makes all that they do more real'.[7]

As you begin to see the world with wondering, not wandering, eyes, and as you begin to observe reality in a radically new way, as a citizen of a new, in-breaking world that you have been welcomed into, your doing will become far more 'real'. It will have purpose, and be inspired by what really lies at your heart. You will see with fresh eyes what truly needs to be done – instead of trying to look busy for the sake of it – and more importantly, you'll see why you are acting. You may find yourself doing less, but with greater energy, power and focus.

Soulful sight

This is not a flimsy excuse for complacency, as John O'Donohue's definition of soul reminds us: 'Soul,' he once said, 'is a bloody dangerous thing to have. It makes you restless, links you into the infinite, whether you like it or not, and won't let you rest happily in your mediocrity and escapism.'[8]

Do you have soul? Perhaps you've never thought about it before. There are many definitions of soul, of course, and as no one can dissect it, or examine it under a microscope, we will ultimately have to work it out for ourselves. But soul might best be described, perhaps, as that place deep within you where your true self meets the divine presence. It is the interface between the person you were created to be and God; the sacred space where absolutely no egoic illusion resides, in which your presence meets the presence of the Creator, links you in with the infinite as O'Donohue says, draws you in and on.

As you give space to your soul, and as you overhear your true self, which communes with the divine, you simply cannot 'rest happily in your mediocrity and escapism', as O'Donohue puts it. Reality becomes something not to be escaped or survived or exploited, but embraced and transformed by your own transforming presence. Reality is not comprised of the soap characters and brand names that populate our minds; it is not houses and cars and the prestige of our jobs. Reality is very different for those with eyes to see.

The last will be first

Reality is a place in which losers become winners and winners become losers, for a start. A place where 'the first will be last and the last will be first'. A place where the poor are, somehow, rich. A place where you do not have to worry about tomorrow, for tomorrow will worry about itself. A place where fear has no hold, and where love reigns supreme.

Reality is an offence to those whose egos strive to look after number one, to win at all costs, to clamber over the bodies of the downtrodden on the way to the top. That's why we're in constant flight from it. But when you begin to see reality through fresh eyes, you begin to see your place within it in a very different light.

The bows and arrows of outrageous fortune

When I was about 10, I went to a summer camp. One afternoon, a group of us were taken to a field to have a go at archery. There was a big box of bows and we were invited to grab one and then collect some arrows. As soon as our instructor had told us to get a bow, the orderly group of kids became a mad scrum. Everyone rushed headlong to get the best one they could. A voice within me told me to wait, to leave the scrum to it and take the one that was left. I obeyed the voice, and stood back until everyone had grabbed what they wanted. As I drew out the last bow, the instructor laughed. 'You've got the very best one,' he said.

Making your presence felt

You are here. Now. Some people never quite grasp that. But those who do cultivate a sense of thankful presence. They stand out. People with presence are those who have learned to live more fully within the present moment. They have a weight to them, a certain indescribable, embodied quality that draws you deeper into their presence. We respond to certain people who have poise, grace, assurance, time, *love* – precisely because they are not trying to be someone or get somewhere; they are simply being who they are, within the infinite now.

Conversely, those who are struggling to be someone, to get somewhere, in space and time, according to the illusions of their ego, will almost certainly cause you to feel unsettled, or overlooked, because their ego is necessarily unsettled.

It's important to stand outside of ourselves to see how others see us – and to see how we can 'be' – if, in each situation we encounter, and with each person we meet, we are to become fully present: attentive, observant, focused, not thinking about other things we need to do, not looking over the shoulder of the person we're talking to (to see if there's anyone else more interesting coming along).

You would love such a person if you met them (they are so rare – that's why they stand out!); yet that person can be you.

It's hard, of course; if you are busy at work and distracted by an unwelcome interruption, you may well not feel like being present to the person who has come to pay you a visit. But you will fare so much better if you allow your self to be fully with them, even if it's to tell them graciously that now is not a good time. Your relationships will deepen, others will appreciate your presence and respond to you more deeply, and your focus will return to your work more sharply.

Childlike wonder

Seeing is all about vision, of course. We often use the word 'vision' in a dull, corporate way to describe what our company or organization is trying to achieve. So often 'vision' becomes an abstract noun and nothing else, written in a paragraph of a website alongside 'values' and left to die a lingering death. Yet vision is really about *how* we see what we see.

And if we have reached a point of no return, in which we see the present with awe and begin to understand the nature of its reality (and our place within it), then we can expect to see things anew, as if through the eyes of a child. If we are to be born again, then we can expect to see things we have never seen before, and wonder at them. If we are to enter a new land, a magical kingdom in which the unexpected is a reality, we can expect to see the unthinkable, the unimaginable, right before our very eyes.

Most of us have grown blind to the colours and shapes of the world God has created for us. We have allowed ourselves to see it through the eyes of our unsettled ego alone. As we enter the present, we will begin to see instead with the eyes of the heart.

Stop to think

How do you see your life? This is absolutely critical to reflect upon. You now have an opportunity to recalibrate your life, and to see it entirely from a different perspective. The eyes of the ego have provided us with distorted vision for the whole of our lives. It is like we have been seeing through a powerful, warped lens.

It may take time for your eyes to readjust. Life may look terrifyingly different when you initially see things with your heart. How have you seen your life up to this point? How does it look different when you begin to see it with your heart?

* * *

Becoming positively disillusioned

As we begin to see with the eyes of the heart, we can become disillusioned – which is good news. We can expect to become disillusioned with the life we have been living, for our illusions will be no more. We often think of being disillusioned as a negative thing. But it's probably the most positive thing to happen to you, in terms of the way you see life from here on in.

It is crucial to remain disillusioned. Every day will be a battle. But if you have reached the point of no return, if you have travelled through the gate, your illusions will become steadily weaker. Your lenses will be removed. Your vision will return to the way it was created to be. As the apostle Paul wrote, 'Do not lose heart… For we fix our eyes not on what is seen, but what is unseen. For what is seen is temporary, but what is unseen is eternal.'[9]

Seeing the mystery

As we begin to see with the eyes of our heart, we must not, however, expect to discover all the answers to life's mysteries. True vision is not about having all the right answers.

We must never stop searching after the truth, for our search for truth is a fundamental part of what makes us truly human. God has set eternity in our hearts, after all. We sense the tug of eternity and our heart responds to the call. But we can be liberated, at the same time, from the addiction of always having to be right, of having the exclusive rights to the answers of life; and we can proceed, unburdened, in the humility of not knowing.

Travel, therefore, with openness: with open eyes, and open hearts. Eyes that are open wide, noticing, observing, watching for the in-breaking world of God, of which we are called to be a part; and open hearts, which are curious, compassionate, wondering, hopeful, gentle, and childlike in their appreciation and delight.

We live within a wonderful paradox, which should never let us become proud: for simultaneously we are all but fools, subject to the constant nagging of our fragile egos, and needing to die to our self; yet we are also children of God. We lose our self to find our self.

We live within a creative tension, and if we keep a close eye on our ego, we can ensure that our vision will remain clear, and pure.

Chapter 15

Living the change

This is the true joy in life, the being used for a purpose you consider a mighty one, the being a force of nature, rather than a feverish, selfish clod of ailments and grievances complaining that the world will not devote itself to making you happy.
George Bernard Shaw[1]

It is no longer I that live…'
Galatians 2:20

In his biography of Mother Teresa, Malcolm Muggeridge noted this about the great woman: 'She gave herself to Christ, and through him, to her neighbour. This was the end of her biography and the beginning of her life; in abolishing herself she found herself, by virtue of that unique… transformation, manifested in the Crucifixion and the Resurrection, whereby we die in order to live.'

He continued, 'There is much talk today about discovering yourself an identity, as though it were something to be looked for, like a winning number in a lottery, then, once found, to be hoarded and treasured. Actually, on a sort of Keynesian principle, the more it is spent the richer it becomes. So with Mother Teresa, in effacing herself, she becomes herself. I have never met anyone more memorable.'[2]

When Mother Teresa allowed her own biography to end, far from slipping into anonymity and insignificance, another, more powerful story began to emerge through her. We reflected in Chapter 8 on the power of story, and it is indeed a truly powerful way of reflecting on your own journey, and passing the wisdom and beauty of that on to others. Yet at this deepest level of spiritual transformation, in our quest to become more truly whole and more fully human, we can strive for something that so few people ever accomplish: the laying down of our own story, and the creation of a divine narrative coursing through us and into the world around us.

In giving her life to the service of the poorest of the poor, Mother Teresa sacrificed her ego, and in so doing, created a scintillating story of what can happen when we give voice to our deeper imagination.

As we stop seeing with the eyes of our egoic mind, we start to see with the eyes of the heart instead. And as we practise using those eyes, we finally come to discover what our hearts can 'imagine' for us; this is a source of imagination we usually keep blocked and locked away, because we are afraid that our heart will draw us away from the security of the fear-driven longings of the ego and into something far more vivid and enthralling instead.

* * *

Stop to think
Where might your own 'biography' end and your real story begin?

Spend time reflecting deeply and powerfully on this. Ask others to help you if you can trust them. What story do you believe your heart longs to tell about who you are and what you passionately stand for? How can you begin to let this story emerge where you are – at work, in your family, with friends…? Where are you prepared to let this story take you?

* * *

Start to act
Try to write something, anything, from your heart. You might like to begin with a period of contemplation, stilling your mind and surrendering the incessant chatter of your ego. Once you have done this, simply write. It might be a story you would like to tell of your life; it may just be a piece of creative prose or an observation. But try to write from your heart, not your head. Where does your writing lead you? (If you do not wish to write, you might prefer

instead to draw or play some music – however you might best express your true self.) How can you best act upon what you have just created?

* * *

Acting truly

As Peter Senge said in the previous chapter, your role is now to become 'present to what is seeking to emerge through you. You move from being an observer to becoming a source through which the future begins to emerge.' Remember the constant relationship between being and doing, as the one refreshes, inspires and invigorates the other in a virtuous circle of hope. As we move through the icons, from seeing afresh into living the change for this final time on our journey, keep reflecting on how your being becomes your doing, effortlessly, seamlessly, in increasing wholeness and integrity.

Our longings, passions, values, dreams are nothing if they are not fleshed out, if they are not *realized*.

First, we realize they are there. And then, we realize them. But what a thrilling way to go: instead of forcing your agenda, you can instead await that which you were previously not conscious of to find its voice and discover its place in your life. Who knows where it might take you? Your actions will become the very expression of your true self, of your heart and soulfulness within this world. You do not need to wait until you get to heaven to begin expressing the previously inexpressible. Life starts now, within this beautifully narrow gap of the present. Enter through the gate.

Communion is a dynamic action, not a passive state

As you let go, you may begin to let come. Or, we might say, you may begin to 'let God'. As you strip back your ego and access that most soulful place in your being, where your true self (with no egoic attachments) is in communion with God, you can discover a place of dynamic being, of constant relating to the Source of life. This is no passive end to your journey, but an active place in which to start relating dynamically. To discover not just who you are, but who God is. Remember, this is not a selfish journey; instead, as you search for God, you search for who you are within God; and as you discover God, you discover the relationship that assures you of your honoured place within the created order, as a child of God.

Richard Rohr says, 'Live in constant choice of God, in constant union with God. Prayer is a daily choice to live out of the Great Self, not the small self; the God self, not the you self.'[3]

Imagine the actions and outcomes that could flow as a result of you truly 'being' and 'doing' without attachment to any ego-driven desires, but instead through a dynamic relationship with the Source and inspiration of life itself!

* * *

Stop to think
How can you imagine acting within such a relationship? What would you *like* to imagine? What surprises may be in store as you let a story emerge through you, instead of forcing one into being?

* * *

Stopping always to overhear yourself

You will never reach that perfect state of what we might call 'flow' this side of eternity. We remain within our fallen state of grace and no amount of self-help or effort will totally unleash our full potential. We have to be realistic, so that we do not become ineffectively idealistic.

That's why it is crucial to maintain the reflective, contemplative life once you start it. Let me give you an example.

Recently, I was asked to give a talk at a prestigious London law firm. I felt very nervous about it as the day approached and I tried to find the right words to say. On the morning of the talk, and before I caught the train, I caught myself feeling increasingly nervous and defensive. Thoughts flooded into my mind about the people I was going to talk to, what they would think, how they would perceive me... And I realized I was beginning to react from the realm of my ego. I was concerned to protect my reputation, and I had begun to focus on trying to *survive* the experience instead of on how I could positively inspire my audience.

But at least I had noticed this; until recently, I may not even have realized what was happening as I tensed up and prepared to go to battle in the wrong sense.

So I decided to stop, and sit in silence, in order to still myself and prepare. And a very strange thing happened. Within a few moments of having settled to sit in silence, I observed that I was singing a song; I was singing out loud, but subconsciously (until I noticed what I was doing!). And the song I was singing was utterly revealing. It was the chorus to a song by Fairground Attraction, which goes: 'It's got to be… *perfect.*'

So there it was. I was driving myself, without even realizing it, to perfection in my own strength. Many of us believe that if our work isn't perfect, we might be found out, exposed, laughed down, humiliated. But that is not the case, of course.

In fact, there is great beauty in brokenness and imperfection. There is tremendous power in standing before people disarmed, vulnerable, fragile and real.

Now that I had truly overheard myself, I was able to lay down my quest for perfection in my talk, and focus instead on delivering something, however imperfectly (for nothing is ever truly perfect!), that would inspire and help those who had come to listen. I was able to make the journey literally and metaphorically towards these people in the spirit of service, and in so doing, I began to relax and know that I had something of worth to impart.

As a result, my talk went far 'better' than if I had been subconsciously striving to prove I was the best (or at least not the worst). Intriguingly, too, I was able to surrender the usual way of 'judging' my performance. Someone shook my hand afterwards and said, 'Very good.' But I took no pride specifically in that – or at least, I took less pride in the comment than I once would have done. I was able to see that in itself, it mattered little whether people were impressed or not, but whether it actually challenged them. And I was able to come away joyfully believing that some people with ears to hear may have been inspired – no more, no less. My reputation mattered little. No one will remember this talk in two centuries' time, or perhaps even in two years' time; but it may just have nudged one or two people into a more open place in which to explore the meaning of their lives.

* * *

Start to act

Next time you approach a task that may afford you some 'recognition' (cooking for a dinner party, making a presentation at work, playing a round of golf, even!), observe how you feel beforehand. Take time to still yourself – not just to quieten your mind, but to overhear what your ego is trying to turn the event into. Once you have identified your fears or defences or insecurities, proactively and deliberately let them go, and approach your task with the freedom to act differently. You may benefit from keeping a journal and reflecting on this process several times, as you practise flowing from your true self.

* * *

Small steps

Mother Teresa famously stated, 'You cannot do great things. You can only do small things with great love.' This is true liberation. As you reflect on how you turn your being into doing, you may feel that this is all too much – that you can't possibly live up to what we are thinking about here. But the good news is that you can; not all the time, of course, but with increasing frequency and effectiveness. And that's because you are not being invited to change the whole world, but to change the way you act within it.

Here, we turn again to the face of love, and away from the place of fear. You cannot underestimate the roles of fear and love in releasing you into a significant, whole state of being. Perfect love casts out fear, as the apostle John once said.[4] Mother Teresa's example brings hope to any of us who feel inadequate, or timid. We can only start small (and presume to continue small). If our focus is on changing the world, we will never do anything. We might 'talk a good game' but at some point we have to step out of the stands and onto the pitch to play.

So instead of thinking big, think small instead. Which everyday actions do you do almost subconsciously? Which parts of your routine could you engage with more lovingly?

Mark Greene tells a wonderful story of the time a famous public speaker came to his house for supper when he was very young. He couldn't remember the occasion himself, but found out many years later that this man – subsequently a hero of his – had once dined with his family. He asked his mother what the man was like: Did he provide a brilliant insight? Did he challenge them in their thinking? Did he inspire them to go out and change the world? His mother simply replied, 'He carved the meat with such grace.'

Mark was perplexed. This wasn't the answer he'd been looking for. A few months after discovering that this man had been to his house for supper, he met him unexpectedly. 'My mother says you came to our house for supper, but the only thing she'll say is that you carved the meat with such grace,' he said.

'Why wouldn't I?' the man replied, quick as a flash. 'That animal had given its life so that we could eat.'

It's the small things we do with great love that demonstrate our own transformation and inspire those around us. True, this great public speaker had a 'platform' in public life, but the integrity of his message flowed through his life in such a way that it determined how he would carve a joint of meat, and made the kind of lasting impression on his host that no amount of words could ever have achieved.

We need to start thinking small, not big. It's only when we attend to the small things in love that the broader sweep of our life will begin to be transformed, after all.

Simple acts of beauty

There is beauty in a small act performed in great love. The Jain monk and peace activist Satish Kumar remembers that when he was young, his mother, a good seamstress, made a beautiful shawl for his aunt. His aunt was so thrilled with this object that she announced she would display it on her wall, rather than wear it, because it was too lovely to risk damaging.

'I have made it for you to wear,' replied his mother. 'It is not for show. So wear it, wear it! Learn to make beautiful and useful things, which are durable, so that when the old ones begin to decay, new ones are ready.'

Kumar recalls, 'The walls of our house were bare, but everything we used – pots, beds, tools, shoes, and other objects of daily life – were well made, and beautiful. Beauty was intrinsic.'[5]

We should try to perform every small act with an inner beauty that shapes our story and brings beauty to others. We cannot capture beauty, as we have already thought about earlier in this book. But we can release and demonstrate it, to let it flow through every small thing that we do and create.

* * *

Start to act

Which small acts of your own could you perform with intrinsic beauty? Is any act too small? If not, choose one thing you do regularly that seems insignificant, and resolve to imbue it with the beauty that lies within your own heart as it communes with God.

* * *

Making your mark

Satish Kumar's mother made a mark on those around her not by stamping her ego on the world – if she had, she would have wanted that shawl to be displayed for her own sense of glory and satisfaction on a wall. Instead, she left a mark of beauty on the everyday life she lived, and on the lives of those around her.

When we live from the ego, we struggle to make an indelible mark on the world so that we might be remembered. Remember, the ego tries to create an indestructible sense of identity for us through its fear-driven urge to survive within a hurting world.

When we live from the true self, we are released to act *within* the world, not *on* the world. It's like leaving footprints in the sand. We cannot help but leave a trace of who we are and where we've been, but we must be prepared to let our footprints fade on the beach of life. Once the tide comes back in, those traces will be washed away. Why do you wish to leave a more permanent sign that you were here anyway?

Instead of hoping that our actions will point to us and cement our identity for posterity in the minds of those who come after us, we might, instead, desire that our actions point beyond us, towards love, or beauty, or God – the things that really matter. These are the things that will inspire and equip others to live and act in beauty and love, and with the light touch that helps us to act truly within the world, instead of harshly upon it.

* * *

Start to act: random acts of kindness
Random acts of kindness and beauty can help us to live spontaneously and with a spirit of generosity. There are even websites devoted to them. Next time you stop to pay a toll at a road or bridge, try paying for the person behind you, if you can afford it – not for the feeling of warmth that you will inevitably receive yourself, but for the feeling of surprise and wonder that the people behind you will experience.

As you begin to look for opportunities in which to perform random acts of kindness, you will begin to see great potential for bringing joy to others and tripping both them and you out of the usual routine of your self-centred life.

* * *

My yolk is easy

A life of generosity should not be a burden but a joy; after all, the more you give to others, the lighter your own load will be! But God loves a joyful giver, says the apostle Paul;[6] and as your actions begin to flow through who you are – giving yourself to others, instead of trying to make things happen for yourself – you will discover a lightness and generosity of being that brings liberation. This is a journey of unburdening, after all; not of accumulating more things to have, or to have to do. And the journey will lead you towards an ease of 'doing' things that is in flow with your 'being', in a way that you may previously not have experienced.

Think of the Ten Commandments God gave to Moses, for instance. You may previously have thought of these as a set of unattainable rules – a burden of law, if you like, that simply proves our inability to live the holy life. You shall not steal, you shall not murder, you shall not covet your neighbour's belongings, you shall not commit adultery...

As you begin to detach from your ego-driven attachments, and live from your true self in communion with God, yourself and others, these commandments become statements of release. You *shall* not covet your neighbour's belongings, because you have been released from the false self that drives you to compare yourself with other people and find yourself wanting.

As we've thought about before, this is simultaneously the hardest journey of contemplation and action that you can ever make in life and the easiest. As you fight like a warrior to make time, to make space, to see with the eyes of the heart and to discover your higher cause, at the same time you will discover an ease and a lightness that specifically unburdens you from all the harmful expectations of the ego-driven world around you. You will be free. Free to live and love like never before. Free to work with joy and energy, through the good days and the bad. Free to love, despite how your mind is telling you you're feeling, and how your emotions are reacting. Free to live on the blade of the moment, with a sharpness that comes from nurturing true presence. Free at last.

Integrity

As your actions emerge through you, as you begin to let go and let come, then your mind, body, heart and soul will begin to align more fully. Released from its incessant chattering, your mind – recalibrated in relationship to your heart – will become more like the razor-sharp tool it was created to be in the first place. This is no mindless journey.

Your heart – uncovered, recovered – is more ready to lead you into action than it ever has been. You are aware of, and in tune with, your body, the whole physical you, and as a result you can experience calmness and assurance, becoming more *embodied*. And your soul can be open to let your true self commune, moment by moment, with the divine source of all life.

God has placed eternity within your heart, and you are drawing ever closer to living within the infinite moment that eternity really is and was from the beginning. The waiting and yearning – which most of us have thought could only be fulfilled in some eternally distant place in the future – can in fact draw us with increasing intensity into the breathtaking beauty of the here-and-now, the every-day.

Born through pain and into pain, our mission is to journey on towards wholeness, our 'being' and 'doing' meeting like partners in a dance of grace. As we make that journey, we do so not in isolation, but as part of a greater whole – a part of the wholeness of God, our selves, each other and Creation – the great unfolding story in which we are invited to play our incomparable part and to let intrinsic beauty flow like a river to those who need it most.

Chapter 16

Passing it on

Being here is so much.
Rilke[1]

We are here. We are wildly and dangerously free.
John O'Donohue[2]

Pinch yourself

Being here is indeed so much. When was the last time that you truly stopped simply to appreciate 'being here'? (Maybe you need to pinch yourself.) Can you remember what you discovered when you did? In this book, we have barely started to scratch beneath the surface of what it means to be here, and to be here now. We have barely begun to glimpse what it means to live with presence, in the present, and to divest ourselves of the things that hinder.

Yet we are, full of the potential to be 'wildly and dangerously free', and to fight like a warrior to win that freedom for ourselves and those we love. There is more freedom to grasp than we can ever quite imagine, but it is our job to try. We are at liberty truly to become wild and dangerous as we seek to imagine and then realize such freedom, to be and to act in love.

As we end the journey through our four icons and four levels of depth, our thoughts turn briefly and finally to passing on the benefits of our travels to those around us – both to those who are already awakened to the vivid possibilities of their existence and to those who remain asleep.

Longing to touch the eternal

Now is the time – for now is always the time – to allow the sense of the eternal present to expand within us, and to fill and flood us with light. God has given us soul; he has placed within us the capacity to be spiritually intelligent and to be transformed as we discover a deep sense of peace and purpose, assurance and relationship, self and selflessness.

We live within the here and now, and our aim is to live so much more fully within it. And yet we must also acknowledge with humility that we continue, as the apostle Paul said, to see through a glass darkly. For we also live within the 'now but not yet'. We will not fully understand until God brings us all the way home. We will never reach a zenith of enlightenment until then. We will never banish pain. In fact, as we move from a place of acute fragmentation towards greater wholeness and a greater sense of our humanity, it is through the *way* that we travel – the way we negotiate the pain and the incomprehension of our human condition – that we will become more fully human. We live within paradox and creative tension. And we live within mystery. Life is not a problem to be solved, as we have acknowledged. It is an unfolding mystery, of which we are a unique part.

As we awaken, we begin to look around us and observe. As we see things differently, we respond through our actions. As we act in beauty and love within the small things, the world around us begins to change for good. That is all, in a sense, that we can do. But we can do it with all our heart, spurred to act in love.

You are you; I am me. God has made me this way. I have tried through my ego to go my own way; you have tried, with yours, to replace the treasure of your heart with fool's gold. We have conspired to cover our eyes and slip into an insipid, banal way of functioning; but we may yet conspire to fight with all our heart against our torpor. We may yet find active, dynamic communion with each other, so that we can release each other's hearts and together act justly, love mercy and walk humbly. We may yet discover what it means to be in constant union with God as we cease to strive in our own strength and begin, instead, to let go and let God come.

Friendship

In today's world, we are more connected than we ever have been. We are networked to the max. Yet the majority of our connections and networks simply conspire to maintain the ego-driven pursuit of social and material comparison. We vie for position, we use others to get ahead, we skim the surface of each other's lives and we collectively maintain the pretence that we all have to keep moving to keep up.

Even on the social networking web site, Facebook, we compete to see how many 'friends' we have, creating a virtual popularity contest if we're not careful in which we collect souls without ever stopping soulfully to meet them or meet their needs.

As we reflect upon 'passing it on', we can awaken to the joy and possibility of our own soul drawing alongside others in sacred, mystical companionship. After all, one of the greatest gifts of God is true friendship.

We have, like so many things in this life, devalued this gift, neglected its possibilities through our own busyness or our pursuit of what can benefit us most. Yet the path of spiritual intelligence reminds us that friends are so much more than just gym buddies or work mates or coffee-morning companions. Friends have the potential to bring us alive and awaken the possibilities inside of us.

Soul friendship

The ancient Celts has an understanding of the 'soul friend', the *anam cara*. The phrase 'soul mate' as it is used today has come to mean a romantic lover with whom we click deeply. But the *anam cara* is something much deeper: a teacher, a companion and a spiritual guide; someone who provides you with a deep sense of recognition – that you *are* here, and that you can be understood without mask or pretension – and belonging.

'When you really feel understood,' John O'Donahue writes, 'you feel free to release yourself into the trust and shelter of the other person's soul.' The *anam cara* is a divine gift, one to be treasured. That's because friendship is 'the nature of God', he suggests – modelled perfectly for the Celts in the Trinity of Father, Son and Spirit. And so a friend is a loved one who 'awakens your life in order to free the wild possibilities inside you'.

Ultimately, he suggests, it is within the embrace of the God who knows us truly, and who offers eternal friendship, that we can 'dare to be free'.[3]

The friendship you are able to offer others, therefore, can be seen in this divine life-light: it reflects something (however dimly) of the true nature of God, as a gift; and within any relationship you have, there lies the potential for you to recognize the true self of others, to help them belong, to awaken wild possibilities and to inspire them to dare to be free.

Small friendship

Remember what Mother Teresa said about performing 'small acts of great love'. The same must apply to our friendships. We cannot befriend the world. But we can befriend small numbers of those around us and demonstrate great love to them. Of course, there are plenty of people around us who we don't even like and who we'll never be true friends with, to whom we can show love through small acts of mercy, grace and acceptance. Neither should we always simply seek friendships with those who are most like us (or who remind us of ourselves!); strangers, as we have considered, can be a great gift if we choose to receive them. But to our friends we can offer – and receive – the intimate embrace of each other's soulfulness.

Our friendships help love to flow through us and between us, and love is the greatest demonstration of reality and presence that we can ever hope to offer and experience. As God is love, the presence of God flows between us, and envelops us, when we act in love. Just as our souls can touch the divine source of life in dynamic, flowing communion, so we can allow ourselves to flow with each other, offering the presence of God through small acts of great love within community.

In loving others, without judgment, seeing them through the eyes of the heart and not the ego, we can release them to be who they truly are – freed from unhelpful expectation or critique, freed from moral judgment or condemnation, freed from the unimaginative and the banal. Pablo Neruda said, 'You are like nobody since I love you.' We are at liberty to liberate each other, to be and to become our made-in-the-image-of-God selves, if we dare – if we dare to imagine, if we fight *for* their hearts and not *against* their minds.

* * *

Stop to think
When were you last happily surprised by a small act of great love from a friend? What happened between you? How did it affect you?

When did you last surprise a friend with a small act of great love? How did it affect them?

When do you sense the presence of love flowing most strongly within your friendships? What is it about those times, in particular, that summons this presence?

* * *

Again, let's remind ourselves that we cannot expect perfection; we live within a fallen state of grace in which we all fall short, continually, of the life which we were created to live. Friendships, however, cannot be judged by their absence of pain, even though we like to do so; we should not simply seek to create anodyne relationships in which we all get along and don't cause any fuss. Friendships are frequently forged in the crucible of pain. They grow deeper through the way we react to unexpected circumstances, to misunderstandings, to wrong accusations, short tempers, insensitivities and oversensitivities. We experience pain when we grow; and we experience pain through the process of birth and (thus) new birth too. Friendships bring into being – flesh out – the mystery of life itself through the mystery of our communion with others.

We bring freedom to life through our awareness of death

Though we so rarely dare to admit it, we are only a short time here. We are indeed 'passing through'. We do not yet see clearly the place from which we arrived before birth; neither do we see clearly where we are going when we experience our re-birth through death.

Nevertheless, we may become more fully aware that we are but a few breaths on this beautiful earth, and thus live accordingly – safe from the fear that we have so much to lose. We do not. And it's our duty, as we enter such awareness, to help 'pass it on' to those around us – to those who, like us, have struggled in vain to see with the eyes of the ego how they can create an unforgettable identity by attaching to as many things as possible while they can. As you begin to lose those attachments, you realize you have nothing to further lose, and everything to gain. That's when we can inspire our communities to live more fully in a state of graceful surrender, as we seek to live with the reality of death – a reality that brings freedom to life.

'Though I walk through the valley of the shadow of death, I will fear no evil,' writes the psalmist.[4] We have probably all heard those words recited at funerals, and they bring us great comfort. But they are not words for the dead alone; they are words for the living. We need fear no evil as we begin the journey into new birth and new life now if we do so with God; and when we are freed from such fear, we are liberated to live with each other in more generous, assured and self-giving relationships.

When a baby is born, it is ejected from the apparent safety of the womb, propelled into the blinding light of day from the darkness it has always known, its umbilical cord to its former life severed. Yet this is its start, its birth. We might look on death in a similar way. The light on the other side may seem blinding to those of us in darkness; we may wish to cling to the familiarity and safety of the womb of our life, and we may flinch at the prospect of having the cord to our former life cut. Yet we are simply moving, if we choose to accept and not fight or reject it, fully into the realm of God's presence, the eternal now, the pure presence of timeless grace and love that we have, as yet, but glimpsed within the pain of our fractured lives on earth.

Growth

As we journey deeper into the mystery of our own being and doing, we will begin to grow. Many of us like to measure 'success' in today's driven culture by sales or profit, through graphs and charts, or by charting how far we have come; but when it comes to personal growth, it is harder to quantify. Instead, we experience a qualitative change that may be subtle, almost invisible to the naked eye; especially if we begin at first to grow by subtraction, losing our attachments, laying down our ego-driven compulsions, putting to death our former selves. And so we must try to see our growth through the eyes of our heart, once more, and not the eyes of our ego.

Remember that Jesus used seemingly ordinary or insignificant images or metaphors to describe the kingdom of God, the new world into which we can enter and play our part, and from which we are invited to derive our identity and claim our citizenship. He described the kingdom as a seed, which grows into a tree that provides shade and in which birds take shelter.

And so, we might like to see our own 'progress' in terms of organic growth, like a tree. Trees are full of presence, of course, seeking to be nothing other than what they were created to be. They seem static; yet they are always growing, and strengthening, and experiencing seasons of birth and death, of seeds and leaves and fruits and shedding and bareness.

Recently I was walking in a wood. In the middle of my narrow path was a man-made barrier, diverting me around a huge beech tree that stood ahead. It was winter, and the tree looked lifeless; a few fallen branches lay on the floor. There wasn't a leaf to be seen. But the sign on the barrier asked people to give the tree an especially wide berth because 'it provides an especially rich habitat for all sorts of wildlife at this time of year'.

* * *

Stop to think
If you think of yourself as a tree, what sort of wildlife are you supporting in your branches and at your base? Who looks to you for support? Who – without knowing it – shelters in your shade?

How able are you to stand tall and strong, safe and assured in the knowledge that you do not need to try to be anything other than who you were created to be?

How do you cope with seasonal change? Do you welcome each season, or are there some that you fear? Are you able to embrace the bareness of winter in the knowledge that life goes on, and that even your broken branches form a vital part of the ecosystem around you?

How content can you be (and become) to grow at the pace that is right for you? Are you ever guilty of trying to force the pace for the sake of growth itself? Do you ever catch yourself wishing you could be the biggest and tallest tree in the wood? If so, try to re-imagine your self the way that God sees you – not by celebrating your size or beauty for the sake of it, but for the part you play within the whole, and the organic beauty you contribute to the life unfolding around you.

* * *

Life is organic, not mechanic. Yet in our mechanized world, we often resort to mechanical metaphors to describe who we are and how we fit together. Recently in the UK, politicians have spoken of it being a 'broken society'. The trouble is that if we see ourselves in mechanical terms, we simply believe that we if fix what's broken, we'll be OK.

Yet as D. H. Lawrence wrote in his poem 'Healing':

> *I am not a mechanism, an assembly of various sections.*
> *And it is not because the mechanism is working wrongly*
> *that I am ill.*
> *I am ill because of wounds to the soul…* [5]

If we look to a more organic way of seeing both ourselves and the others around us, we have to appreciate the fact that life flows through us and between us; that we are all inter-related, placed within Creation as part of a whole.

The apostle Paul used the metaphor of the body to help and inspire his readers to understand how they inter-relate within God's in-breaking on earth, within the reality of love and presence that truly forms our relationships. No part is more or less significant than another, he observed. All have their role. And if one part is suffering, the rest of the body feels its pain.

No man is an island, as the poet John Dunne wrote. No woman, either. We are intrinsically linked to each other, through the pain and joy of being human, and of being created within a created order. We pass on pain if we are hurting; we transmit fear palpably if we are fear-driven. And we pass on the best of ourselves – if we are assured, generous and self-giving – like a contagion of hope, an irresistible revolution of love as the author Shane Claibourne so beautifully describes it, through who we are and what we can begin to imagine we can really do for each other.

Going well

Spiritual intelligence is a useful way of thinking about who we are and why we're here. God has given us the soulfulness to reach out within the present to embrace the gift of eternity that he has made available to us. This is not just for holy people, or religious people, or mad people. We all have spiritual intelligence and anyone can begin to realize their potential through it. As Evelyn Underhill wrote, 'We cannot say that there is a separate "mystical sense" which some men have and some men have not, but rather that *every human soul has a certain latent capacity for God, and that in some capacity is realised with an astonishing richness.*'[6]

By accessing your spiritual intelligence, uncovering your soul, discovering your heart, putting to death the false self and welcoming the true, you will unleash a thousand practical manifestations as you become more fully present to your self and those around you – more alive to your tasks, more observant, poised and ready for action. You will begin to reflect powerfully, discover who you truly are, sense the presence and grace of the divine source of life and enter a whole, new way of being.

But these are mere descriptions, signposts on the journey. The icons and ever-deepening journeys simply help to inform; the great challenge is to fight like you've never fought before – against banality and the false self, and for life and love in all its fullness. It is the hardest of journeys, and the easiest. It will take great courage and tenacity, but your journey will not be completed in your own strength. You will find yourself by losing yourself. You will know life, even as you begin to die to the person formerly known as you.

There is a season for everything, says the writer of Ecclesiastes. 'A time to be born and a time to die; a time to plant and a time to harvest... A time for war and a time for peace.'[7] We might add a time to contemplate and a time to act. Here we come alive, soulfully rediscovering what it means to become more fully human, more fully ourselves, and more fully God's – found and lost within the creative tension of the great mystery of life itself, awakening daily to its myriad possibilities, seeing through awestruck eyes, living the change with all the wildness and danger of someone with nothing to lose, and passing it on simply because you cannot help but do otherwise.

Life starts now.

It is an astonishing privilege.

Being here is so much.

Pinch yourself.

And go well.

> *It doesn't have to be*
> *the blue iris, it could be*
> *weeds in a vacant lot, or a few*
> *small stones; just*
> *pay attention, then patch*
>
> *a few words together and don't try*
> *to make them elaborate, this isn't*
> *a contest but the doorway*
>
> *into thanks, and a silence in which*
> *another voice may speak.*
> **Mary Oliver**[8]

Notes

Introduction

1. Underhill, E., *The Mystics of the Church*, James Clare & Co., 1987, p. 11.

2. Zohar, D. and Marshall, I., *Spiritual Intelligence: The Ultimate Intelligence*, Bloomsbury, 2000, p. 9.

Chapter 1

1. de Mello, A., *Walking on Water*, The Columba Press, 1998, p. 62.

2. Eldredge, J., *The Journey of Desire*, Thomas Nelson, 2001, pp. 191–92.

Chapter 2

1. McGregor, J., *If Nobody Speaks Of Remarkable Things*, Bloomsbury, 2002, pp. 1–2.

Chapter 3

1. Gladwell, M., *The Tipping Point*, Little, Brown and Co., 2001 (paperback ed.), p. 13.

Chapter 4

1. John 8:6–7

2. Matthew 5:13–14

3. Psalm 1:3

Chapter 5

1. Coupland, D., *Hey Nostradamus!* Flamingo, 2003, p. 33.

2. Eldredge, J., *The Journey of Desire*, Thomas Nelson, 2001, pp. 191-92.

3. Matthew 6:28–29.

4. Ecclesiastes 1:2.

5. Kerouac, J. *On the Road*, Penguin, 1991 ed., p. 57.

6. 1 Timothy 6:10.

Chapter 6

1. Fox, M., 'The Hidden Spirituality of Men', *Ode Magazine*, October 2008, Vol. 6 Issue 8, p. 60.

2. Tolle, E., *The Power of Now*, Hodder Mobius, 2005, p. 37.

3. Tolle, E., *op. cit.*, p. 92.

4. Riddell, M., *The Sacred Journey*, Lion, 2000, p. 144.

5. Gibran, K., *The Prophet*, Oneworld, 1998, p. 23.

6. Fox, M., *op. cit.* pp. 60–64.

Chapter 7

1. Okri, B., *In Arcadia*, Phoenix House, 2002, p. 226.

Chapter 8

1. Okri, B., source unknown.

2. Peterson, E., *Eat This Book: The Art of Spiritual Reading*, Hodder and Stoughton, 2006, p. 40.

3. Taylor, D., *Tell Me a Story: The Life-Shaping Power of Our Stories*, Bog Walk Press, 2001, p. 1.

4. Bass, R., quoted in Gruber, P., 'The Four Truths of the Storyteller', *Harvard Business Review* December 2007, p. 56.

5. Gruber, P. *op. cit*, p. 59.

Chapter 9

1. Extract from 'Something in the Woodshed', interview with William Paul Young by Brian Draper, *Church Times*, 14 November 2008, pp. 22–23.

2. Chambers, O., *My Utmost for His Highest*, Dodd Mead & Co., 1935, entry for 29 September.

3. Tolle, E., *The Power of Now*, Hodder Mobius, 2005, p. 14.

Chapter 10

1. Dicarlo, Russell E., in Tolle, E., *The Power of Now* by Hodder Mobius, 2005, p. 18.

2. Lewis, C. S., *A Grief Observed*, Faber and Faber, 1966.

3. Acts 9:1–19.

4. Rohr, R., extract from lecture notes.

5. O'Donohue, J., *Anam Cara*, Bantam Press, 1999, p. 15.

6. Psalm 24:1.

Chapter 11

1. Lawrence, T. E., *The Seven Pillars of Wisdom*, Penguin Classics, 2000

2. Millman, D., *The Way of the Peaceful Warrior*, H. J. Kramer, rev. ed., 2000, p. 15.

3. Peck, Scott M., *The Road Less Travelled*, Arrow, 1990, p. 46.

4. Riddell, M., *The Sacred Journey*, Lion, 2000, p. 87

Chapter 12

1. Greenspan, M., *Healing Through the Dark Emotions*, Shambhala, 2003.

2. Extract from Stanford Commencement Speech 2005. Available online: www.youtube.com/watch?v=D1R-jKKp3NA.

3. Mark 8:36.

Notes

4. Micah 6:8.

5. Riddell, M., *The Sacred Journey*, Lion, 2000, p. 64.

6. Hart, H., 'Open Hands, Open Heart', *Ode Magazine*, Dec 2008.

Chapter 13

1. Millman, D., *The Way of the Peaceful Warrior*, H. J. Kramer, rev. ed., 2000, p. 9.

2. Borg, M., *The Heart of Christianity*, HarperOne, 2004, p. 50.

3. Genesis 28:12–16.

4. Eldredge, J., *Waking the Dead*, Thomas Nelson, 2006, p. 27.

5. Matthew 6:21

6. Senge, P., Jaworski, J., Otto Scharmer, C. & Flowers, B., *Presence: Exploring Profound Change in People, Organizations and Society,* Nicholas Brealey Publishing 2005, p. 160.

7. Mark 1:15.

8. Matthew 13:31–32, 44–46.

9. Matthew 19:24.

10. John 3:7.

Chapter 14

1. Underhill, E., *The Mystics of the Church*, James Clare & Co., 1987, p. 11.

2. Senge, P., Jaworski, J., Otto Scharmer, C. & Flowers, B., *Presence: Exploring Profound Change in People, Organizations and Society,* Nicholas Brealey Publishing, 2005, p. 93.

3. Tolle, E., *The Power of Now*, Hodder Mobius, 2005, p. 52.

4. Ibid.

5. Millman, D,. *The Way of the Peaceful Warrior*, H. J. Kramer, rev. ed., 2000, p. 166.

6. Underhill, E. *op. cit.*, p. 11.

7. Ibid.

8. O'Donohue, J., in an interview conducted by Brian Draper, 'The Business of Spirituality', www.churchtimes.co.uk/content.asp?id=44571.

9. 2 Corinthians 4:16, 18.

Chapter 15

1. Shaw, G. B., 'Dedicatory Epistle', *Man and Superman*, Penguin, 1950.

2. Muggeridge, M., *Something Beautiful for God*, Lion, p. 17.

3. Rohr, R., extract from lecture notes.

4. 1 John 4:18.

5. Kumar, S. *You Are, Therefore I Am: A Declaration of Independence*, Green Books, 2002, p. 33.

6. 2 Corinthians 9:7.

Chapter 16

1. Rilke, R. M., from 'The Ninth Elegy' in Rilke, R. M., *Duino Elegies*, (Cohn, S., trans.), Caracanet Press Ltd, 1989.

2. O'Donohue, J., *Anam Cara*, Bantam Press, 1999, p. 271.

3. O'Donohue, J., *op. cit.*, p. 35–39.

4. Psalm 23:4.

5. Lawrence, D. H., *The Collected Poems of D. H. Lawrence*, 1928.

6. Underhill, E. *The Mystics of the Church*, James Clare & Co., 1987, p 11.

7. Ecclesiastes 3:2–8.

8. Oliver, M., 'Praying' from *Thirst: Poems by Mary Oliver*, Beacon Press, 2006, p. 37.

To find out more information about Brian Draper's work with spiritual intelligence,
visit www.web.me.com/echosounder